Susan Hale

A Family Flight through Spain

Susan Hale

A Family Flight through Spain

ISBN/EAN: 9783744756150

Printed in Europe, USA, Canada, Australia, Japan

Cover: Foto ©Andreas Hilbeck / pixelio.de

More available books at **www.hansebooks.com**

THROUGH SPAIN

BY
Miss SUSAN HALE

Author, with Rev. E. E. HALE, of " A Family Flight through France, Germany, Norway and Switzerland," and of " A Family Flight over Egypt and Syria "

FULLY ILLUSTRATED

BOSTON
D. LOTHROP & COMPANY
FRANKLIN STREET

NICHE IN THE ALHAMBRA.

CONTENTS.

	PAGE
CHAPTER I.	
OVER THE BORDER	13
CHAPTER II.	
DIVIDING FORCES	22
CHAPTER III.	
TO BURGOS	28
CHAPTER IV.	
THE CID	35
CHAPTER V.	
THE CATHEDRAL	42
CHAPTER VI.	
A LONG NIGHT	50
CHAPTER VII.	
MADRID STREETS	58
CHAPTER VIII.	
HISTORICAL	67
CHAPTER IX.	
AN INCIDENT	74
CHAPTER X.	
THE VAUGHANS	83
CHAPTER XI.	
CALLE ISABEL, 16	93
CHAPTER XII.	
TOLEDO	102

CHAPTER XIII.
Visigoths.. 111

CHAPTER XIV.
Combination.. 120

CHAPTER XV.
Cordova... 130

CHAPTER XVI.
Andalusia... 138

CHAPTER XVII.
Early Spain... 147

CHAPTER XVIII.
Sevilla.. 156

CHAPTER XIX.
Another Cathedral.. 163

CHAPTER XX.
Justa and Rufina.. 172

CHAPTER XXI.
Italica... 179

CHAPTER XXII.
Murillo.. 189

CHAPTER XXIII.
Cadiz.. 196

CHAPTER XXIV.
The narrow Strait... 204

CHAPTER XXV.
Malaga.. 211

CHAPTER XXVI.
The Conquest of Granada................................ 220

CHAPTER XXVII.
The Alhambra.. 232

CHAPTER XXVIII.
More of the Alhambra.................................... 243

CHAPTER XXIX.
The Generalife.. 249

CHAPTER XXX.
The City of Granada.. 258

CHAPTER XXXI.
Bessie to Mary.. 265

CHAPTER XXXII.
The Picture Gallery... 275

CHAPTER XXXIII.
Spanish Art... 283

CHAPTER XXXIV.
King Alphonso... 292

CHAPTER XXXV.
Perro Paco.. 303

CHAPTER XXXVI.
Napoleon in Spain... 311

CHAPTER XXXVII.
Philip's Adventures... 324

CHAPTER XXXVIII.
Zaragoza.. 332

CHAPTER XXXIX.
Barcelona... 343

CHAPTER XL.
Out of Spain.. 350

LIST OF ILLUSTRATIONS.

Niche in the Alhambrà	*Front.*	Bridge of St. Martin, Toledo	76
A Placid Party	15	Hospital of Santa Cruz, early	
Bordeaux	18	16th Century	76
Biarritz	20	Zocodover in Toledo	81
A Wine Merchant	21	Santa Maria la Bianca	85
Bayonne	23	Empty Wine Jars	88
A Basque	24	Six-Mule Team, Toledo	89
Battle between Bayonne and the Basques	25	Alcazar	92
		Bridge of Alcantara	93
Spanish Mule-bus	30	Donkeys carrying Water Jars	94
Outside the Stable	32	Looking back across the Bridge	95
The Fruit Merchant	34	Puerta del Sol, Toledo	97
A ragged Hidalgo	36	In the Water Cellar	101
Courtyard	38	Procession of Monks	103
Coffer of the Cid	40	The Cathedral of Toledo	107
A Spanish Scene	41	Map	111
Patio of a Spanish Inn	43	Roman Gateway	113
Interior of a Spanish Cathedral	47	Alcazar in Toledo	115
One of the Bells	48	King Wamba	117
Omnibus with Mules	50	Omnibus to the Station	119
Flowering Aloe	51	Roman Tomb	121
Spanish Milk Jugs	53	Puerta de la Inclusa	123
Madrid in the distance	54	Cervantes	126
Royal Palace, Madrid	55	Ancient Entrance	127
A Shoemaker	57	A Mountaineer on his way Home	129
Coat of Arms	58	Coat of Arms of Cordova	130
Puerta Del Sol	61	Entrance to the Orange Patio	131
Cooling Drinks	64	Interior of the Mosque of Cordova	133
El Buen Retiro	65		
The Spanish Devil's-fiddle	66	Charles the Fifth	134
Fountain of Neptune	68	Wall of the Mosque of Cordova	135
Ferdinand the Seventh	70	Bridge over the Guadalquivir	136
Christina	71	Moorish Knocker	138
Isabella the Second	72	Church of San Pablo, Cordova	140
The Vegetable-dealer	73	Raphael's Pillar	141
Coat of Arms of Toledo	74	Patio of a private House, Cordova	143

List of Illustrations.

"Buenas Dias"	146	
Andalusians	147	
Arms of Seville	148	
Manola	148	
Andalusian Serenade	150	
Fountain in the Alhambra	152	
Balcony in Seville	153	
Deserted Square	157	
Cathedral Gate	159	
Giralda	160	
Giraldilla	161	
Ornamental	162	
Interior of Cathedral	164	
Puerta del Perdon	165	
Holy Mother	166	
Seville Housetops	167	
Torre del Oro	169	
Gardens of the Alcazar	170	
Spanish and Moorish Scenes	171	
Fountain in the Alcazar	174	
Moorish Arches, Alcazar	175	
La Sala des Embajadores, Alcazar	176	
Roman Amphitheatre at Italica	181	
Palace of the Duke de Montpensier	184	
Garden at San Telmo	185	
Leaves from a Sketch-book	188	
Murillo	190	
Nuns at Prayers	193	
At an old Well	195	
Alguazils	197	
A Lady of Cadiz	199	
Old Amateur	201	
Cadiz from the Sea	202	
The Rock of Gibraltar	206	
Roman Bridge, Ronda	208	
Safety Boat	209	
Arms of Granada	211	
The Cathedral and Port of Malaga	212	
Banks of the Darro	213	
Puerta del Vino	215	
Gypsy Girl	218	
Gate of Justice, Alhambra	221	
Ferdinand and Isabella	223	
Moorish Arches	226	
Dos Hermanas, Alhambra	227	
Arabesque in the Alhambra	230	
A public Conveyance	231	
Plan of the Alhambra	232	
Court of Myrtles	234	
Court of Lions	235	
Window in Hall of Ambassadors	239	
An Event in the Village	242	
Entrance to Hall of Ambassadors	244	
El Mirador de la Reina	246	
Cypress Walk in the Generalife	251	
Glaring Granada	254	
Gypsy Quarter	255	
At the Gates of a Town	257	
Tomb of Ferdinand and Isabella	259	
Elizabeth dictating her Will	260	
House in Granada	262	
Palms at Elche	263	
Postilion	265	
On the Vega	266	
Spanish Balconies	268	
Parting at the Station	269	
Spanish Diligence	271	
In a Village	274	
Interior of the Armory	276	
The gridiron-shaped Escurial	278	
Library of the Escurial	279	
The English Elms, Aranjuez	281	
Showing their Love for Music	282	
The Dwarf "El Primo"	285	
Velasquez	287	
From Equestrian Portrait of Philip the Fourth	288	
Paul Rembrandt	289	
The Amateur	290	
Equestrian profile	291	
Prince Balthazar Charles, son of Philip the Fourth	293	
Entrance to Botanical Garden	295	
State Carriages	296	
Royal Stables	297	
Cooling Drinks	298	

List of Illustrations.

Old Spanish Embroidery	299
Gate of Hospicio	301
Torreros entering the Arena	303
Torreros before the Café de Paris	305
Picadors preparing for the Combat	306
A fair Spectator	308
Orangé Boy in Arena	309
Outside View of the Arena	310
Charles the Third	311
Monument of the Dos de Mayo	312
Driving the Bulls down	313
Velarde and Daoiz	315
The Espada	316
The Arena	317
Carrying off the Victim	321
End of the Contest	323
Arms of Zaragoza	324
Luz	325
Cirque de Gavarnie	327
Manuel Molina	328
A Relay	330
The Bridge at Cordova	331
The Leaning Tower	333
Old Courtyard	335
Ox-team of Aragon	336
The Colegio de Procuradores, Zaragoza	337
Cathedral, Barcelona	341
Catalonia Cart	344
Prison of Inquisition, Barcelona	346
Gigants	347
The Battle of Lepanto	348
Arms of Barcelona	351
Montserrat	353
Live Stock	354
Port at Marseilles	357
The Signal	359
Marseilles again	360

A FAMILY FLIGHT THROUGH SPAIN.

CHAPTER I.

OVER THE BORDER.

"ABSOLUTELY nothing, sir, but wearing apparel, and perhaps a few drawing materials."

This statement in French was made to a mild-looking official who stood within a long counter piled with trunks, boxes, portmanteaux and valises. On the outer side was an anxious crowd of travellers pressing and pushing to find their own impediments, in order to have them passed without delay.

The mild official chalked a white cross upon the box under inspection.

"Is that all, Monsieur?"

"That is all, Bessie, is it not?" asked the gentleman who was conducting the transaction; "one, two, three and the ship trunk," he added in the same breath.

"No, papa, I have not found the little black box yet."

"Here it is!" cried a boy who now appeared, bumping every one in the crowd with the corners of a small travelling box which a porter in a blue blouse was struggling to take away.

"This man cannot speak anything," cried Tommy, "but he thinks the trunk belongs to those other people."

Blue Blouse consented to surrender the box; by this time the mild official was far away on his side of the counter, making white crosses upon the boxes of other impatient tourists, some of whom were obliged to open their trunks to satisfy the inspectors. All the travellers who were to go away by the train which was standing outside the station, were in a great hurry; all the officials who were to stay, appeared to be in no sort of haste.

Finally one of them turned his attention to the little trunk. It was a harmless black box, marked T. P. H., but for some reason it appeared suspicious to the Spanish inspector, and he demanded that it should be opened. Straps were unfastened, the key produced, and the top thrown back. Soiled linen, slippers, and a dressing-case appeared upon the surface. The man plunged his hand into a corner, fumbled about, punched and squeezed a sponge in its india-rubber bag, then withdrew satisfied; and the party, now permitted to return to their seats in the train, hurried through the long room where many other people less fortunate than themselves were still searching for their effects, and undergoing the examination, which, however slight it may be, is always tedious and vexing. They passed along the row of carriages, some of them empty, the doors standing open ready for their occupants who were still away struggling with the inspectors. In others, placid parties were reading or chatting together. A lady sitting at the open door of a compartment, was watching for the party; as they approached she called out:

"Here I am! I have guarded our seats like a dragon, and I believe we shall still have the compartment to ourselves. Is everything safe?"

"Yes, aunt Dut," replied the girl. "And here are your keys. We did not have to open one of your things, and they only fell foul of Tommy's small box."

"I don't care," said the boy, "they did not find the rahatlicum; it was too near the bottom."

A PLACID PARTY.

"You do not mean to say that any of that is left!" exclaimed MISS LEJEUNE.

For this was Miss Lejeune who was guarding the carriage, keeping seats for the rest of the party, which consisted of herself and Mr. Horner, with Bessie Horner and Tommy. These now all entered the carriage and began to dispose of the wraps and straps which they had spread about upon the seats before leaving it, in order to make the aspect of things as forbidding as possible to passengers searching for seats. A compartment in continental railway carriages is built to hold eight, but it is much more comfortable for four persons only; thus it becomes one of the great arts of travel to keep out intruders. Four is the most convenient number for a party travelling in this way. It not infrequently happens that they can keep a compartment to themselves, and have plenty of room for putting up feet, leaning comfortably in corners, and above all, they can control the two windows. There is room for the exhibition of all grades of good breeding, and bad manners, in this matter of the compartment. It is perfectly fair for a party to try to keep the whole for themselves, especially if the train is long, with plenty of accommodation for all; it is annoying when new-comers persist in invading the place already taken possession of, and, by trampling upon toes, crowding the racks, and pushing themselves into the vacant seats, succeed in making the whole journey uncomfortable, and their presence disagreeable, instead of seeking elsewhere in the train an empty carriage. On the other hand, perhaps the intruders have not been able to find another carriage, or are forced to take this one by the guard, who does not encourage the exclusive system; in this case, it is hard for the late arriving travellers, flustered and hurried, with their hands full of rugs and bags, to find themselves most unwelcome, with no space resigned to them, only forbidding glances cast upon them, and even grumbling remarks which they can guess at well enough, although the language in which they are spoken may be foreign.

The Horners were now settling themselves into the best corners of a first-class carriage of a train which had just crossed the frontier between France and Spain. The station was Irun, in the Spanish Basque Provinces. At Hendaye, their last French town, they had crossed the frontier, and there changed carriages, necessary because the Spanish railways are built with a wider gauge than the French one, in order to impede invasion, it is said. Judging by the length of time required to transfer the ordinary travel of a period of peace, we may imagine that the delay to an impetuous army might be serious.

The Horners had left Bayonne about noon that day, having come from Bordeaux the day before. The day was lovely and the scenery charming, with glimpses of the Bay of Biscay, at intervals, on one

BORDEAUX.

side, and on the other the soft line of the receding Pyrénées. It would have been pleasant to linger at Arcachon, a bright watering-place near Bordeaux, or to take a branch train to Biarritz, the favorite resort of the Empress Eugénie, still beautiful, though less frequented than in its palmier days. As they crossed the little river Bidassoa, which is the boundary between France and Spain, they saw a small island *les Faisans*, called also *l'Ile de la conférence*, which has served as neutral ground for more than one meeting important in history, as for instance the exchange of Francis the First, of France, after he had been the prisoner of Charles the Fifth.

"See!" said Miss Lejeune in a low tone, nudging Bessie, "there are those people who came from Bayonne. I saw them passing before. I suppose they have been identifying their boxes."

"They look nice," replied Bessie, "but I am glad they are not coming in here, for they have such quantities of hand-baggage."

"They must be changing their seats. Perhaps they did not find good ones at Hendaye."

The party they were observing consisted of a tall elderly gentleman, and three ladies, of whom the first seemed advanced in middle age, while the other two, who followed, were much younger, one of them wearing her long hair in a braid, as Bessie still did, for convenience in travelling. Each of the party was laden with shawls, umbrellas, guide-books hastily seized upon at a sudden signal for flight, and a waterproof of india-rubber trailed on the ground from one of the overflowing heaps. Tommy jumped out and ran up to the youngest girl, saying in French:

"*Permettez moi, mademoiselle,*" while he tried to take her third umbrella from her.

"Oh, thank you; don't trouble yourself," she replied in very good English.

They had now reached the door of an empty carriage, and Tommy's assistance was by no means superfluous in helping them in. A little shriek, however, from the engine, startled them all, and he left them to hurry back to his own party. The guard pushed him in, banged the door, hurried every one else on the platform, banged more doors, and waved his hand at other guards banging other doors.

"Now we are off," said Bessie, leaning back in her stuffed and cushioned corner.

After this, the train stood motionless on the track for more than twenty minutes; useless to inquire wherefore. Nothing of importance occurred. The luggage had been all examined and marked and transferred to the vans. No passengers were missing. The Horners put their heads out of the window, but saw nothing to account for the delay. The Spanish passengers in the other departments were not disturbed, but quietly read their newspapers and smoked their cigarettes.

Thus it is upon the Spanish railways. Repose and procrastination pervade the system. Perhaps the officials inherit from Moorish

BIARRITZ.

ancestors the Mohammedan belief in "Kismet," for it is by Faith and Fate that trains reach their destination, rather than by rule and time-table. They start sometime, and they arrive somewhere, and that is pretty much all that can be asserted of their punctuality.

For the rest, the carriages are comfortable and clean, the officials are civil and obliging, the *buffets* frequent enough, and the food good enough for travellers with good digestions, and enterprise, to risk experiments in strange cakes, fruits and beverages.

After all, there is no hurry! If you have allowed a certain time for seeing Spain, you may as well see it from a railway station as elsewhere. The Horners, like other Spanish travellers, came to feel more intimate with the two gens d'armes, or alguazils, who stand at every station, than with any other inhabitants of the country. They stand immovable, in full uniform, with white hats that have a sort of flap at the back, watching the train, and awaiting its start. They are always on the platform as the train draws up at each station, and they all look so exactly alike, that it is pleasant to indulge the belief that they really are the same pair transferred by some process of swiftness, as yet unknown to the rest of the Spanish, from one station to another, to protect with their wooden vigilance the interests of the travelling public.

·A·WINE·MERCHANT

CHAPTER II.

DIVIDING FORCES.

SPAIN is entered perhaps most naturally in the way the Horners selected, by crossing the frontier at Irun, in order to pass down through Burgos to Madrid. It was now the first of May, and, although they had made all haste in coming from the East, where they had been passing a delightful and instructive winter, the season was somewhat advanced for making the Spanish trip.

"Spain so late!" exclaimed the Wiseacres. "You will perish with heat."

"You never will be able to stand the climate of Madrid in June."

"Make haste to get through the southern part first, or you will miss all the charm of it," said others.

In spite of these discouraging warnings, the Horners continued to feel an interest in their own plan, which had been made not without recognition of the phenomena of heat and cold, as affected by climate. They came from Bordeaux to Bayonne through the level, monotonous, but picturesque Landes, where Bessie from her window had the good luck to see a shepherd on *chanques* — tall stilts — which are still worn by the people to move about upon the soft, marshy ground. The Landes is a barren stretch of country, covered with turf and moss. Pines are the only trees, and it would look desolate enough, except that where the railway crosses it, trees lately planted are beginning to change its aspect of desolation.

Bayonne is a fortified town, enclosed in walls, and entered by four gates. It is so near the frontier of Spain that it already begins to have a Spanish look. The streets are lively with a great variety of faces, costumes and languages; for Basques, Gascons, and Spaniards, are coming and going continually. The women have pretty handkerchiefs tied about their heads, and the men wear *berêts* and *ceintures* of bright colors.

The Romans constructed a citadel at Bayonne. As early as the

BAYONNE.

twelfth century it was a place of importance for the whale fishery, tanning of leather, navigation, and traffic with Spain.

The marriage of Eleanor of Aquitaine with Henry of England, gave Bayonne to that country. Richard Cœur de Lion extended its privileges, which came to be so great that it was almost independent. Subsequent rulers had much trouble in restraining its liberties. The mayor of Bayonne used to be in those days a most important magnate, executing justice as seemed right in his own eyes, upon all evil-doers. The Bayonne people were always at odds with the Basques, their next neighbors, and intimate enemies; legends remain of endless contests, and of one great battle in the hall of a town where the Bayonne men were surprised by a party of Basques. They fought with chairs and tables, as well as sharper weapons, until almost everybody was killed on each side.

A BASQUE.

It was at Bayonne that Francis the First arrived from his prison at Madrid, and found his mother and the court awaiting him. Since then the local history of the place may be said to consist of passages back and forth of princes and princesses; in the present century it has served often as a place of shelter for Spanish political schemers.

The Basques, into whose province the Horners now passed, are said to be the descendants of the earliest inhabitants of the Peninsula, and to this day they preserve their strongly-marked characteristics of custom and language. Like the Bayonne men of old, they have a strong sense of independence, and a determination to maintain laws of their own, which have been respected at all times. They are noted for truth and honesty, and for their unbounded hospitality. They are tall, and often handsome, with fair hair and blue eyes. like the ideal Norsemen, which comes naturally from their Celtic origin, different from that of other Spaniards. The Basque language, wholly different from Spanish, is remarkable, and difficult. They still wear the national costume, which is highly picturesque; for the men, short dark velvet jackets, and loose trousers, with *alfargatas* on their feet, and a blue or bright red sash about the waist.

The Horners at once began to enjoy the novelty of the Spanish national costumes. Although, as in other parts of Europe, these are now somewhat superseded by the encroaching black broadcloth for men, and conventional Parisian fashions for women, much still remains of picturesque attire. Each province of Spain has its own characteristic; different colors prevail in different places, with, however, a general similarity. The short breeches coming only to the knee, with buttons up the outside of the leg, are so much more becoming to the manly form than the long, slouchy trousers enforced by fashion, that it seems strange that man's vanity should have been so passive as to allow the change. Alfargatas are sandals of white hemp, thick and strong, for the sole of the foot, bound on with a mysterious arrangement of strings, generally black, crossed over the foot.

It must now be explained why the Horner family is so small as to occupy only the four corners of their compartment. They have been

BATTLE BETWEEN BAYONNE AND THE BASQUES.

seen filling the whole of one without extending the actual limits of their party.

Upon leaving the East, Spain was the goal towards which the minds of the Horners turned, but there was a difference in the degree of longing with which each regarded that land of romance and sunshine. Mrs. Horner expressed a willingness to do it vicariously, and a preference to settling down somewhere quietly, while the rest of her family went through Spain; after which they could come back and tell her all about it. This idea was only accepted with equanimity by the rest because it seemed reasonable. It was quite unlike the last division of the family, when the broad Atlantic and the narrow Mediterranean had flowed between the two parts. A large party is inconvenient for travelling anywhere, and especially in Spain; not only for comfort in railway carriages, but by diligence, in hotels, indeed, in all manner of sight-seeing.

Mrs. Horner received the full permission of the council to "form a nucleus" where she liked, and to select her companions who were to remain with her, leaving four to undertake the Spanish campaign. She chose the Pyrénées for her retreat, with ample advice from the friendly Fords, who knew the region well, where to select her point of repose. Mr. Horner she appointed leader of the Spanish expedition, and Miss Lejeune his chief counsellor, keeping Philip as her own protector, escort and financier. Between the two girls it would have been difficult to select, but that Mary seemed hardly strong enough for the undertaking. Everybody depicts the condition of Spain as so deplorable, its roads so bad, its inns so poor, that there is a general impression that only giants for strength, and lions for courage, should undertake it. Mary herself hesitated, fearing she should be an encumbrance; at times not up to the requisite mark. Bessie on the other hand was now in full health and spirits, with a tremendous appetite, and unflagging powers of endurance. She smelled the battle afar, and champed the bit; it would have been cruel to have deprived her of it. So Mary stayed behind with her mother. Tommy became number four, and very joyfully.

Mr. Hervey was out of the reckoning for either branch of the party. He accompanied them all to Marseilles, and thence to Lourdes, a way-station on the way to Bordeaux, where the great separation took place, the Spanish portion going on to Bordeaux, and thence to Bayonne, as we have seen, while the rest took a branch train up to Pierrefitte, among the mountains. Mr. Hervey still escorted them, wishing to see them fairly settled before he left them for America.

They had a couple of hours to wait at Lourdes, where is the famous "Grotto of the Virgin." A close row of omnibuses waited at the station to convey people to the Grotto, and small boys waylaid every one on foot, with voluble offers to escort them thither; but the Horners were not even tempted by simple curiosity to avail themselves of the opportunity of seeing the immense church which has lately been erected on the spot where, in 1758, the Virgin Mary is said to have appeared in person to a young girl. There is a fountain of supposed miraculous powers of healing, and thousands of pilgrims visit the place. Since the miracle has been pronounced "authentic" by the Church, it is wholly given over to their accommodation, and to making money out of them.

A fine drizzling rain made the landscape dull, and the roads muddy. Mrs. Horner and Mary preferred to remain in the station reading guide-books and newspapers which they bought at the bookstall, while Mr. Hervey and Philip, with some difficulty escaping the attacks of tormentors, determined to take them to the Grotto, found their way up to an old castle picturesquely placed on top of a little hill.

"What are you smiling about, Mary?" asked her mother, across the top of the *Vie Moderne* which she was looking over.

"Poor Bessie!" replied May. "I was thinking of the last thing she said while we were standing on the platform before their train went off. She is so afraid she shall not be up to the mark about the Spanish galleries. She said: 'I know I shall not like the right things, and then aunt Gus will be dissatisfied. She will miss you all the time she is looking at the pictures.'"

Mrs. Horner laughed, but said:

"Bessie has very good taste in pictures. I dare say she will do very well."

"But she has heard of the Montpensier collection which came to Boston long ago, and she fears all Spanish pictures are horrid."

CHAPTER III.

TO BURGOS.

AT last the train was fairly off, and the Spanish Horners, as we must call that branch of the family who were to explore the Peninsula, settled themselves in the four corners of their compartment, which was, luckily for them, all their own. They were such old travellers by this time that everything proceeded with a certain system. Four neat shawl-straps seemed of themselves to seek commodious corners of the rack above their heads. Four umbrellas fell together behind the straps. There was, besides, a small straw box containing lunch put up at Bayonne, and a little book-strap which held the guide-books and time-tables.

It will be observed that each one had an individual shawl-strap and umbrella. This can hardly be avoided in travelling, and it is a good plan for each person to consider himself absolutely responsible for these two things of his own. It was the rule with every Horner, but, for the first time on this trip, Tommy, grown both strong in arm and chivalric at heart, announced to Miss Lejeune at the outset that he meant always to carry her strap as well as his own.

It may seem to tarry-at-home travellers a want of gallantry on the part of the gentlemen, that the ladies of the party should ever be allowed to carry their own straps; but experienced tourists know that the leader of a party must not be burdened with even the thought of such things. It is the responsibility more than the dead weight of hand-luggage which makes it a burden; for in general there is not much carrying to be done; a stout porter is almost always to be found upon whose broad shoulders portmanteaux may be heaped, and whose hands hold all possible parcels. He carries everything faithfully and accepts at the end fifty centimes, or its equivalent, with contented cheerfulness.

So Miss Lejeune, accepting, for the boy's sake quite as much as her own, this gallant knightship, was not encumbered with wraps. As soon as they were started, Bessie undid the little book-strap.

"Which will you have, aunt Gus?" she inquired.

"Give me O'Shea, unless your father wants it."

"Not at all," replied Mr. Horner. "I am going to devote myself to accounts, for I have not yet accustomed myself to this Spanish gold."

At Bayonne Mr. Horner had exchanged his French money for Spanish without difficulty; nor did he find it difficult to understand the latter, it is so like the French, a *peseta* being worth somewhat, but not much, more than a franc. The sum he received was given him chiefly in bright gold coins worth twenty-five pesetas each, looking very much like English sovereigns, and of about the same value. The *reales* were rather puzzling to the Horners, because they heard a great deal about them, but only saw pesetas and countless small coins of trifling value, which they never came to clearly understand. Hotel bills are generally reckoned in reales, and as it takes four reales to make a peseta (twenty cents), the number at the bottom of a bill looks formidable with its sum of figures until it is divided by four, after which it subsides to a moderate number of pesetas with nothing alarming about it.

A real is about the same as five cents; but it seems a more important value in Spain, on account of the number of lesser coins, sometimes very small in size, for one of which may be bought in the street a handful of carnations, or an immense magnolia blossom ten inches in diameter.

The time passed quickly as the train swept along through scenery sometimes grand and wild, suggesting bandits and brigands. The guide-books kept our party well posted on the points of interest, historic and romantic, and they would have been glad to pause often to make a sketch or inspect a castle. Darkness alone gave rest to their eager eyes, and minds excited with this first experience of Spain. They were glad to sit silent for an hour or two. It was ten o'clock in the evening before they arrived in Burgos.

Here they left the train, with all their little Spanish phrases at their tongues' ends, ready to do battle in that language. Passing

SPANISH MULE-BUS.

out of the station, and surrendering their tickets to the man at the gate, they saw a long line of omnibuses, and a long line of porters, all labelled — both men and carriages — with the names of their several hotels. This was quite as it would be elsewhere in Europe, and quite reassuring. Mr Horner, however, endeavored to give a Spanish turn to the way he pronounced the words *Fonda del Norte*. The man whose hat was encircled with the same words, took them to the omnibus of that hotel, took the small piece of paper, which in Europe corresponds to our bunch of baggage-checks, and by and by returned with their effects, which were hoisted up to the top of the omnibus, and plunged down upon it with the usual thump. All this was all *en règle*, except that the vehicle seemed a little squarer and squalider than some they knew, and Tommy had perceived that three mules in a row were harnessed to it. The two or three people who joined them were evidently not Spaniards, but travellers like themselves — a grumbling Frenchman, and a very stout German with a curved nose. They started off with a jerk, and cracking of whips. The three mules kicked up their heels, as Tommy could see through the darkness from the little front window, and they were whirled off over a rough pavement, at a mad pace. The passengers were bumped against each other, the windows rattled, the little kerosene lamp smoked and smelt, the thing rocked as if it would tip over. As they could not in the least see where they were going, it was a little alarming.

"I'm glad mamma is not here," said Bessie, holding on to the side of the omnibus, "if it is all going to be like this."

"I like it" — much, Tommy was about to add, but the sudden jolt of stopping shook his mouth together before he had time to finish his sentence.

They were ushered into a low, dimly-lighted passage-way. Two or three proprietors and waiters, both men and women, came out to receive them, and Mr. Horner bravely began to state his views about rooms, in words culled from several Spanish conversation-books. "*Quatro camas y quatros por quatro*," was what he had learned by heart, a troublesome collection of q's and c's, which means "four beds, and rooms for four." He was greatly relieved, though not flattered, to be answered in English, which, though not of the best, was more intelligible than his Spanish. They were soon shown to a wonderful *salon*, low and large, furnished with dingy chairs and furniture, sofas, a shabby carpet, clocks and mirrors after the manner of France, dimly lighted by two candles. From this opened at each end a bedroom, so that Miss Lejeune and Bessie on the one hand, and Mr. Horner and Tommy on the other, were comfortably established. Two truly Spanish maids came in, with *panuelas* round their heads, and bustled about the beds.

OUTSIDE THE STABLE.

Miss Lejeune began trying her Spanish on them, and said, in that language, that she wished much to learn to speak it.

"Poor lady!" said the girl to her companion. 'The Señora wishes to speak our tongue, and she cannot."

After they were refreshed a little they went up-stairs to supper, or late dinner. Their own rooms were up one flight from the street, and were directly over a stable, whence the sounds, and eke the odors, of animals arose, and in the morning the cheerful hee-haw of a dear donkey. There was no grand entrance or broad corridor to this hostelry; all the stairs looked like back stairs, and the passages were dark and narrow. They were placed at one end of a long table, filled with guests, chiefly men, all apparently chance travellers. The table was lighted by hanging lamps (probably kerosene), and ornamented with vases of mature artificial flowers. The courses were served at the elbow, like any other *table d'hote*.

So much is said and asked about the food in Spain, that perhaps it will be well, once for all, to give a little account of it. It is known, by this time, that the Horners were never fastidious about what they ate, and that they had failed seldom to discover wholesome food, in some form, wherever they went. They were prepared to find things pretty bad in Spain, and therefore were agreeably disappointed in this matter. The fact is, that now almost all hotels in large Spanish cities, are kept either by French or Italians, and the food is much the same as that furnished in other hotels on the Continent; better or worse, according to the grade of the hotel. This dingy old Fonda at Burgos differs from the hotels of Madrid and Seville, in being less like those of other continental towns; so that the little bit of Spanish experience which the Horners had had at the outset was not repeated for some time.

A real Spanish dinner begins with a soup, good or bad, according to the cook who makes it. *Puchero* follows inevitably, the national dish *par excellence*, and always served. It is not very different from the "boiled dish" of New England, being boiled meat, surrounded with vegetables, and garnished with slices of sausages, lard, and ham, with tomato and saffron, and red peppers, for even in the food local color glows, as in everything else Spanish. The chief ingredient is *garbanzos*, which Gautier describes as "peas striving to appear to be beans, in which they are only too successful." *Puchero* is not bad; it is eaten with alacrity at first, but after being served week in and week out every day and perhaps twice a day, it palls upon the palate, and one reason for being glad to get out of Spain, is seeing the last of it.

Eggs cooked in oil — good fresh oil — which is used much instead of butter, or some slight *entremet*, follows the *puchero*, and then comes fish, at this odd point in the meal. After this the inevitable roast and salad, sweets and cheese, on this occasion the excellent *queso de Burgos*, a specialty of the place follow, with delicious fruit, oranges, strawberries, or apricots, according to the season.

CHAPTER IV.

THE CID.

UNDER their heads were the omnibus-mules in their stalls, but nevertheless the Horners slept sound in their first Spanish bed. Before they slept, they heard the call of the night watch, ending with "All's well!" at first faint in the distance, then after a pause, louder, and then dying away again repeated far off. This reminded them of Alexandria, and made them feel quite at home.

Next morning instead of coffee, there was brought to their rooms a tray containing cups of thick chocolate, and bread, with a tumbler full of water for each person, and resting across the tumbler a long piece of crisp white sugar, called *azucarillo*. This is the national morning meal, and our party was resolved to adopt the national habit. The chocolate was good, but very thick. "Too filling, for this time in the morning," said Miss Lejeune, and after this experiment she went back to her favorite *café au lait*, which can always be had fairly good. Tommy rejoiced in the chocolate, and in the sweet azucarillo, which should be eaten after it is dipped in water. A glass of water inevitably follows a cup of chocolate. It is supposed to aid the digestion of it. Miss Lejeune thought it would take more than a glass of water, of which she was not fond, to settle the rich heavy beverage, especially so early in the morning, and she seldom tried chocolate after this. This was an exception to her general rule of always eating in Rome as the Romans do.

When the maids came in to make the beds, the Horners were still in their salon writing letters. Bessie after careful research in her conversation-book, asked of one of them at what time would be *almuerzo*,— breakfast.

"Allassonzas," replied, apparently, the maid.

"Gracias," said Bessie, lisping the c with Castilian elegance. She was half encouraged, half mortified at her Spanish attempt; evidently she had been understood, for she received a prompt reply, but what under the sun was it!

"Allassonzas!" she repeated as soon as they were alone. They knew their numbers pretty well, but this sounded not like any of them.

"I'll tell you," she herself exclaimed, "it must be eleven! Onza is eleven, and they probably say á las onzas, at the elevens!"

"Whereas we were at sixes and sevens," murmured her papa, showing that he was in the best of spirits, since he permitted himself a poor pun.

A RAGGED HIDALGO.

They decided to go out and explore the streets until almuerzo, and reserve the Cathedral for the long afternoon; so they sallied forth, Miss Lejeune armed with her sketch-book, sighing for Mary who was always her companion in this pursuit.

Every step brought something amusing before their eyes. The very beggars in Spain wear their cloaks like hidalgos. They were constantly meeting Don Cæsar de Bazan and all his family.

"Tommy! You ought to draw. Stop! I will give you this extra book and some charcoal. You must!"

"I cannot sketch," said Tommy sheepishly; but he took the things, and afterwards made a very good attempt at a dog sitting down.

They all established themselves in an old arched doorway, looking through at a picturesque court. Mr. Horner kept guard, and Bessie sat by with a book, though she did not read much, while Miss Lejeune rapidly washed in effects in water colors.

They were soon surrounded by half the town of Burgos; not only boys, but women with babies, and grown men, and above all, dogs, who pushed in close to them to investigate, and were recalled by their owners; the crowd behaved very well, and expressed themselves in half whispers, of which the first word intelligible was "perro;" they said it so often, and the dogs advanced so often, that the travellers soon put their ideas together. Bessie pointed at a dog and said inquiringly, "Perro?" "Si Señorina," replied the ragged boy, and smiled a smile Murillo has often painted, showing all his Spanish teeth.

The favorite hero of Spain is the Cid, Rodrigo Diaz de Bivar, the most prominent figure in Spanish literature. The name is so obscured by myth and fable as to be almost lost to history. No doubt such a man lived, but so many impossible deeds have been ascribed to him, that it is hard to select the true ones. There are, indeed, a Cid of history and a Cid of romance, very different from each other, but both exerting a singular influence in developing the national genius.

The Cid of history is still the hero of the early period of the struggle between Christian and Mohammedan, and a good type of the Spanish Goth of the twelfth century. Rodrigo Diaz, better known by this Arab title of "the Cid" (el Seid, the lord), was of a noble family. The date of his birth is uncertain, but it was probably between 1030 and 1040, during the reign of Fernando the First, a great and wise prince, under whom the tide of Moslem conquest was first checked. He possessed a large dominion in Spain, but on

COURTYARD.

his death it was divided among his five sons. Castile fell to one, Leon to another, and other provinces to the rest. Not long before, the Moorish possessions had been broken up into numerous petty states, and hence there was quarrelling of every description, — between brother and sister, between Castilian and Galician, as well as between Christian and Moslem. No condition of affairs could be more favorable to the genius of a warrior. The Cid first rose to distinction in a contest between two Sanchos of Castile and Navarre, in which he won his name of Campeador, — the champion, — by slaying the champion of the enemy in single combat. After this, he was entrusted with high commissions, and fought many a battle for his king, then Alphonso the Sixth; in 1074 he was wedded to Ximena, a royal princess. The original deed of the marriage contract is in existence. But his great prowess and many successes raised up enemies who found it easy to kindle the jealousy of the king. He was accused of keeping back for himself part of the tribute he had won for the king, who took advantage of his absence on a raid against the Moors, to banish him from Castile.

Henceforth Rodrigo begun upon the career which has made him famous, fighting on his own account, sometimes under the Christian banner, sometimes under Moorish and sometimes against both. Among his enterprises, the most famous was that against Valencia, which he took, after a nine months' siege, in 1094. This was the richest prize snatched from the Moors, for Valencia was then the most flourishing city on the Peninsula. The Cid took it for his own kingdom, and ruled it according to his own will, with vigor and justice, for four years. At length the party of the Moors most powerful at that time, the Almoravides, whom he had several times beaten, marched against him in great force, and his army was crushed. The blow was a fatal one to the now aged and war-worn Campeador, and he died of grief and anger, in July, 1099. He was buried in a monastery in the neighborhood of Burgos, with his wife Ximena. There, in the centre of a small chapel, surrounded by his chief companions in arms, still rest, after frequent disturbances from friend and foe, the bones of this mighty warrior, the genuine Spanish hero, the embodiment of the virtues and vices of his time.

Philip the Second made an effort to have him canonized, but Rome objected, and not without reason. Whatever were his qualities as a fighter, the Cid was not of the right material to make a saint,— a man who battled against Christian and Moslem with equal zeal, who burnt churches and mosques alike, who ravaged, plundered and slew for a livelihood as much as for any patriotic or religious purpose, and who was, in fact, about as much of a Musselman as a Christian in his habits and character.

This is the Rodrigo of history. The Cid of romance, of legend and drama, is a different character, invested with all the attributes of a grand hero. He is the type of all knightly virtue, the mirror of patriotic duty, the flower of all Christian grace. He is Roland and Bayard in one. From the time of his actual life he has been the subject of song, and within a hundred years from his death he had become the centre of a whole system of myths. The celebrated poem of the Cid was written in the latter half of the twelfth century; there are hundreds of ballads relating to him, some of them full of simplicity and fire. His horse Bavieca, and his sword La Colada, are as famous as himself.

Although the glory of the Cid spreads all over Spain, it is at

COFFER OF THE CID.

Burgos that the interest in him centres, since it is there that he was born, and there that his bones actually repose. When the Horners were going through the Cathedral, they were shown in a side chapel a heavy wooden coffer supported high up against the wall upon iron brackets. It is a worn-out, worm-eaten old box, and looks like the grandfather of all trunks. This is the celebrated *Cofre del Cid;* one of two trunks which he once left as security

THE CID.   41

with a Jewish banker, for a loan of six hundred marks, assuring them they contained all his jewels and gold, but that they were not to open them until his return. The true contents of the boxes were sand and rubbish, heavy enough to deceive the bankers. If he came back and paid the sum he had borrowed, this was all very well; there is no proof that he ever restored principal or rendered interest, but we will hope that he did so.

Tommy asked why the coffer was thus suspended on high, and the guide told him it was to keep it out of reach of too eager tourists and admirers of the Cid, who could not resist splitting off little bits of the wood as mementos, when it was within their reach.

CHAPTER V.

THE CATHEDRAL.

WHILE they were eating *almuerzo*, a merry meal in the dining-room above stairs, with a mixed collection of travellers from various countries, all finding fault with the dishes in a variety of languages, Miss Lejeune said, "If each one of our fellow-guests had what he wishes to eat set before him, what a mixed *menu* it would make!"

"Yes!" exclaimed Tommy; "liver, sausage and macaroni and baked beans and edible bird'snests."

"O come, Tommy, there are no Chinese here!" said Bessie.

"No, but very likely some one would order it for a delicacy."

"Quite raight, my young friend," said a stout German next Tommy, who understood a little English, and thought he could speak it; "most peoples shall tink him own dish what most nasty to all nations."

The sentiment was good, although obscured by its imperfect expression. Tommy controlled his face, and waited till they had all left the room before he repeated the sentence to his family.

After very good black coffee, the Horners sallied forth to see the Cathedral, through the picturesque streets, always admiring the groups of beggars. They surrendered themselves, though reluctantly, to a guide, as they had not much time to spare. Such a guide is at once the stay and torment of sight-seekers. He pesters them with gabble, drags them to see things they do not want to see; he makes them stand staring at worthless relics, and tears them away from the contemplation of a masterpiece. He is ignorant of art, history, men and manners, and yet assumes superiority

PATIO OF A SPANISH INN.

over travellers because he knows, and they do not, the way around his one cathedral. It is delightful to dispense with the services of any guide, and driving off the swarms of them that come buzzing about, to explore the intricacies of a town, a church, or cathedral, according to one's own sweet will; then every new object seems a discovery, snatched from the whole collection of wonders. The tourist can make his own decision upon the merits of a work of art, and follow undisturbed the thread of thought it awakes. This course can best be pursued when there are several days to be spent in one place, and time enough to spare for the loss of it, which is sure to come from turning the wrong corner, mistaking the point of view, and thus dilating with the wrong emotion.

A wily old *valet de place* leads his victims straight to headquarters. He really does know best what they wish or what they ought to see, indeed, the thing that makes him so disagreeable is that he does know more than they do. Then he has keys to locked-up chapels, or can procure them, and he knows the shortest way round the building. The quickest way is to surrender to him entirely, go everywhere he suggests, believe everything he says, for the moment. This was the Horners' plan up to a certain point, when often after a tramp of several hours, they sometimes "bolted" unexpectedly, and, to the astonishment of the hitherto flattered guide, absolutely refused to stir another step, demanding to be restored to their hotel.

Matters reached no such extreme at Burgos. They found their way alone to the Cathedral easily, and there fell into the hands of a mild, mechanical man who could do a little routine English. He trotted them round the place, showing everything, and was neither too loquacious nor too persistent.

The Cathedral of Burgos is undoubtedly one of the finest in Europe; a grand specimen of the thirteenth-century Gothic. If, since it is the first Cathedral studied, after entering Spain from Bayonne, it is overlaid by other impressions in the mind of the tourist who presses on to Andalusia and the wonder of Seville and Grenada, yet nevertheless, in the quiet hours of repose when the journey is over, the vision of it comes back in all its force and purity.

The towers and pinnacles are open work, and in the distance they are seen against the blue sky like filigree work, and at night stars can be seen through them. The Cathedral is somewhat shut in, as it is built on uneven ground, surrounded by poor little houses; and the Archbishop's palace is so close to it, as to form, as it were, a part of the same building; and on the opposite side a good impression of the inward arrangement can be had from the outside.

After studying for some time the innumerable statues of angels, martyrs, warriors and princes which adorn the façade, our little party entered the immense building, and stood silent before the grandeur of the interior. It was impossible to do more at first than to look silently around, following the lines of the columns, and curves of the arches, while a vague delight and wonder came filling the mind.

After a little while Mr. Horner came nearer to Miss Lejeune, and said softly:

"This is the real thing!"

"Oh, yes!" she replied. "It satisfies all my requirements for a Spanish cathedral."

It was many minutes before they felt inclined to do more than to move about, receiving, without analyzing, the effect of the vast proportions of the whole, graceful at the same time, and harmonious, until the guide became impatient, and they followed him about to the different chapels, each itself like a church, in richness and variety. In each is entombed some great personage, with his recumbent statue extended in the middle, the head upon a pillow, and the hands clasped upon his breast, — priests clothed in their festival robes, warriors in armor, princesses in regal attire; and all surrounded with a profusion of carvings, gold decorations covering the walls, altars and ceilings; every chapel contains an army of angels and saints cut in marble or wood, painted, gilded, clothed.

It is this splendor and richness of decoration which distinguishes the cathedrals of Spain; gold, color, carving, and everywhere, and yet there is nothing either gaudy or tawdry in the effect, for all at the same time is sombre and grand, perhaps because the proportions are so large, but more because it is all genuine work. After the solemn sincerity of these cathedrals, at the same time full of richness and warmth, that of Cologne seems cold and bare, and the decorations of the modern French churches flimsy.

Descriptions of cathedrals are always tedious to those who have not seen them, and it will not do to weary the

INTERIOR OF A SPANISH CATHEDRAL.

reader with a detailed account of all the Horners visited. Their general impression of richness and grandeur lasted all through their expedition in Spain. It was at Burgos that Bessie first removed her idea of "doing a cathedral" from the category of idle sight-seeing, to that of the most thorough enjoyments of travelling.

They looked with wonder at the celebrated Cristo de Burgos, which is said by tradition to have been carved by Nicodemus shortly after the burial of our Lord. It was found, according to the legend, inside a box, floating in the sea, and after many adventures, it finally was brought from this cathedral to a *convent*. It is certainly of very early date, and admirably modelled, with a deep expression of pain; the hair, beard, eyelashes, etc., are all real. With strange taste, the image is clothed with a small embroidered petticoat.

Even Tommy liked this cathedral better than most he had seen in his travels, because as he expressed it, "the side-shows were all first-rate." The clocks of the cathedral are furnished with small figures, which come out as the hour strikes, like the famous one at Berne. About one of these the sacristan told them this legend, in a broken sort of French, which made it more impressive.

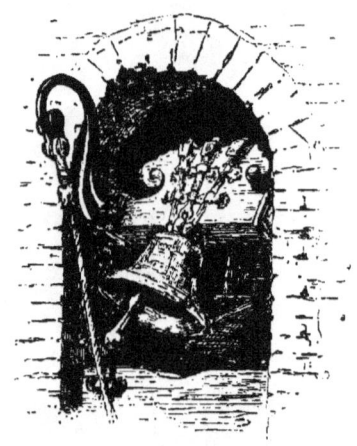

ONE OF THE BELLS.

It was about a king of Spain, Enrique the Third, who lived in the fifteenth century, and a young girl who used to see him frequently in the cathedral, although no word was ever exchanged between them at their meetings.

One day in leaving the church, the young unknown dropped her handkerchief. The king picked it up and gave it to her, when the fair one disappeared and was seen no more. A year after, the king became lost in the woods one time, and was attacked by six hungry wolves; he killed three of them with his sword, but after that he began to feel tired; and he was about to be devoured by the others, when suddenly he heard the sound of a gun, and a strange cry, at which the three wolves fled. He turned round and beheld the young woman he had seen in the cathedral. He advanced towards her, when she said with a strange smile, "I love the memory of the Cid so much that I love all that is great and noble ; thus I have wished to consecrate to you my life. Accept the sacrifice."

As she spoke thus she fell dying to the ground, pressing to her heart the king's handkerchief.

The king, moved by such devotion, wished to honor the memory of his preserver, and hit upon the singular plan of putting an image into a clock in the cathedral, which at every hour should remind him of the cry of the girl in the forest. He wished the figure to repeat the very words she used, but the skill of the Moorish artist of that period was not up to the idea, and he achieved only a puppet of life-size, which made a kind of shriek when its time came. It caused so much amusement afterwards to the irreverent, and disturbance to the faithful, that its springs were broken by the order of the ruling bishop, and ever since the puppet has been silent.

Spain is full of legends and romances, which seem worth listening to on the spot, however absurd they become when transferred from their natural surroundings. The Cid still lives. Roderick the Goth is a fact, and as for the Moors, they assert their rightful claim to the soil everywhere, while Ferdinand and Isabella appear like monsters who drove them from their inheritance. The defects in the Moorish morality are forgotten, and they figure as martyrs to the imagination.

CHAPTER VI.

A LONG NIGHT.

SHORTLY before nine P. M., after another meal in the upstairs dining-room, the Horners climbed again into the mule-bus and started off to the station. They had seen the empty vehicle every time they went in or out of the hotel, for it was

OMNIBUS WITH MULES.

kept out in the street before the door, hard by the mules in their stable under the house.

Mr. Horner, and even Miss Lejeune, were a little low in their minds on account of anticipating the long night journey which was before them. This is the great drawback of travelling in Spain. The through trains all fly by night like bats, and turn and twist as you may, and thumb your time tables o'er and o'er, there is no method of evading the discomfort. The party all had such a passion for looking out of windows at the scenery, wherever they were, that it was a positive loss to them to pass over so much ground in the dark, and this regret was added to the discomfort of a night's journey. However, it was not to be helped. After a little futile inquiry for *wagons-lits*, which are supposed to exist, but which are always on some other line than the one where they are wanted, they settled themselves into their corners, with through tickets for Madrid, facing the prospect of eleven hours and a half shut up in their carriage.

They were all so tired after a day of busy sight-seeing that they felt sure of a good nap to begin with, and so without their usual lively chat, they prepared for the night, opening the straps and disposing of rugs and shawls as best they could in the way of pillows and coverings. Luckily there was no one else in the carriage, as Miss Lejeune observed with thankfulness.

"So I can make myself as hideous as I please," she added.

This she proceeded to do by tying a blue veil tight across her

FLOWERING ALOE.

forehead, and bringing the ends around under her chin, after which she crammed herself back into a corner with her feet up and well tucked in. They had drawn the thin silk curtain across the hole in the top of the carriage through which the gleam came from a dim lamp, but some little light still made itself felt.

"I love to look at you, aunt Gus," said Bessie sleepily; "you look like a mysterious blue sphinx in that corner off there. The veil is very becoming so."

"I am glad you are my only admirer just now," replied Miss Lejeune gloomily.

Tommy was apparently fast asleep in the position with which he had first dropped; but he suddenly exclaimed:

"What has become of the H. family! We saw nothing of them at Burgos!"

"To be sure!" cried Bessie, waked up by the question. "They must be lost. We have not seen them since Irun! Papa, have you seen them?"

"Hm-m-m," was the sole reply of her father.

"Hush, Bessie," said Miss Lejeune; "your father is asleep already."

"Valladolid!" he murmured in a thick and sleepy voice.

"Do you suppose," said Bessie, now in a much lower tone, "that they went on to Valladolid without stopping at all at Burgos? They must be idiots!"

"You don't know, my dear. I believe Valladolid is very interesting, or they may have special reasons."

"She looked like an artist, the tall one," said Bessie; "are there pictures at Valladolid?"

"Do shut up!" barked Tommy; "can't you let a fellow sleep?"

The remonstrance though inelegant was just, and Bessie, without resenting it, closed her lips and eyes at once.

So they all travelled to Madrid through the Land of Nod, for nod it is, with the jar and jolt of the train. All was silence in every compartment as the long train swept through the darkness, occasionally stopping with a jerk at a station, then starting off with another jerk. The four were not often all asleep at the same time. Each had his or her periods of misery, when a change of position was absolutely necessary. There was a twist and a turn, a thumping of pillows, and then the weary head fell down again in a new posture, not better, perhaps, but at least different.

Once they were all awake but Tommy, who slept straight through like a top. They compared watches, and found it was only half-past twelve. The night seemed endless; and when it came to an end, the journey did not. At dawn they bestirred themselves and looked out upon the landscape. It was raining steadily, and the country was wild and barren in the extreme, without verdure or vegetation; huge piles of irregular rocks were tumbled about, with here and there a scrubby pine. Salvator Rosa might have painted a bit anywhere, into which a bandit with his gun would have come very naturally.

SPANISH MILK JUGS.

How the Horners felt is well known to those who themselves have waked up at dawn in a railway carriage with the prospect of several hours more travel. Their mouths were parched, their cheeks hot, their heads dishevelled, their limbs all stiff and cramped; and they were faint for want of coffee or something refreshing. The lunch-box had chocolate in it, dried ginger and a few sweet biscuit; but Tommy was the only one who found these things at all acceptable.

A woman at a station was calling "*Leche! leche!*" and Mr. Horner bought from the window in exchange for a very small coin, a lovely red jug containing goat's milk. He and Tommy liked it, really, but Miss Lejeune shook her head without trying it, and Bessie shuddered after one taste, and took no more.

"How stupid you are not to like milk," said Tommy crossly. Tommy was rather cross, but nobody minded it. They were too uncomfortable to mind it.

"It is milk that does not like me," said Bessie meekly. "I have no objection to it."

As the light strengthened, their spirits rose somewhat by the gloomy interest of the wet and dripping landscape. The famous

MADRID IN THE DISTANCE.

Escorial was passed upon their left, they swept through the last long tunnel, and saw Madrid in the distance, nearing fast, the royal palace crowning the height in front.

The scene at the station was much like any other European experience. Everything showed that they had reached a large cosmopolitan centre. Cabs and omnibuses were in attendance, and they were soon passing through a gateway to ascend the steep hill leading to the town. An official stopped them at the entrance-gate, and fumbled with their hand-bags; but it was only a brief formality, and soon they found themselves in comfortable rooms at the Hotel de la Paix, on the beautiful Puerta del Sol.

"Puerta del Sol," said Tommy, who had recovered all his anima-

ROYAL PALACE, MADRID.

tion and usual politeness. "I thought it was the name of the hotel."

"So did I, to tell the truth," said his father; "or at least my ideas were not clear about it."

"Oh, papa! you must have known that the Puerta del Sol was a beautiful great square," said Bessie.

"My dear," said he smiling, "I have not been reading up on Spain as you have. You must remember I have scarcely looked at a map. This is your expedition and Augusta's."

This conversation was shouted across the omnibus as they

rattled along the paved street, and Miss Lejeune, who never would speak in a noise, smiled and nodded, and significantly patted the little parcel of guide-books and maps which she held firmly in her hand.

It was, in the main, Miss Lejeune who had laid out the plan of the Spanish excursion. She had long longed for the Peninsula. In her youth, long ago, the house of a friend who married a Spanish explorer, was filled with curiosities, which he had brought home, and the acquaintance with these things thus early planted in her mind a strong wish to visit the country; there were engravings from Velasquez, terra cotta images of matadors, mantas of glowing stripes, and *salvers* or beaten brass, all of which helped to make the desire grow. As time went on, she gained an underlying conviction that sometime she was to go to Spain. She trifled a little with the language, and even went through a grammar. The chances which had led her several times over Europe, and to the East, had not been favorable until now, when she was really about to visit her long-established *Chateaux en Espagne*, with those dear Horners, who now furnished her life with its chief enjoyment. She was very happy in being thus able to carry out her dream, and in being allowed to have her own way about it, too.

Miss Lejeune had omitted Valladolid in her plan, as it was wise to press on towards the south before the weather should become too hot. But Valladolid is an interesting place which might well be used to break the long journey from Burgos to Madrid.

It was for a long time the residence of the kings of Castile, and later, in the time of Philip the Second, who was born there, it was the most prosperous city in Spain. It was he, however, who removed the court to Madrid, and this proved a death blow to the prosperity of the deserted city.

The Museum and Cathedral contain some interesting pictures and sculpture. The Cathedral was never finished on the scale intended by Herrera, the architect of Philip the Second, who made the designs for it, and began it, because he was called to Madrid in order to build the Escorial; and when the court went to Madrid, no funds were forthcoming to finish the abandoned Cathedral, and so it was merely put into condition to be used, as it was, for public service. The libraries contain some rare old books; and the streets, like all Spanish towns, are full of picturesque subjects for sketches.

CHAPTER VII.

MADRID STREETS.

COAT OF ARMS.

AN excellent French waiter, with a white cravat, and a napkin under his arm, came to take their orders, — so there was no occasion for Spanish yet, — and soon returned bringing a broad *plateau*, or tray, loaded with refreshing coffee, hot milk, chocolate for Tommy, bread and butter and boiled eggs, for which Mr. Horner stipulated. Although his whole family were fond of the European system of eating little or nothing early in the morning, Mr. Horner retained a secret prejudice in favor of something solid, and, whenever he could, he added *oeufs à la coque* to the order. What was more, he generally found that all the eggs were eaten; more than one, then, must share his secret preference, for Tommy and he could not eat them all. But Miss Lejeune and Bessie, in Spain, kept up the theory maintained by all the rest in previous journeys, that they wished nothing but bread and butter with the coffee. The Hotel de la Paix is a large French hotel. Miss Lejeune and Bessie shared a room with two high beds placed end to end, filling up the whole of one side. Upon a great round table which took up the middle of the room, coffee was served, and Mr. Horner and Tommy joined the ladies to partake of it. Their own room was close at hand, smaller, but with the same view. The large windows all had projecting balconies, from which they could look sideways toward the Puerta del Sol, although the rooms looked upon a narrow side street.

As soon as Bessie had refreshed herself with one cup of coffee, she went to the window and established herself there, roll in hand, that she might lose none of the wonders of the new city while she was eating. All the windows had balconies, and many of them striped awnings. Opposite, and somewhat lower, a barber had a little bird with a red tuft on its head, hopping about with a long string to its leg. Within the room Bessie could see the barber, shaving; but from time to time, he left his customer to come and see the bird, with his cigarette in his mouth; kissed his hand to it, puffed a little smoke in its face, to console it for being tied, and went in again. A hand-organ below was playing charming Spanish dance-music. A still narrower street, a mere lane, in fact, opened nearly opposite them. It was swarming with people in strange colors, and a group had collected at the corner to listen to the announcement of a bull-fight. This was Sunday, and the great square was filled with people, the women with mantillas on their head, and fans in their hands instead of parasols. The fashionable ladies are giving up the pretty mantilla for Paris bonnets, which is a great pity, for a bonnet does not look right on a Spanish fair one; but it is still the rule to wear the mantilla to church, so that in the morning the streets of Madrid are filled with devotional mantillas, while later on in the day only foolish French hats prevail.

Suddenly Bessie called out, "Oh, come! come **quick**!" and the others reached the balcony in time to see the end of a cavalcade of royal guards in white *bournous*, following the king's carriages. Bessie had seen the whole; a string of carriages with outriders, postilions, and much gold ornament, followed by mounted guards. It was his Majesty going to church.

These excitements, however, could not make the travellers forget their fatigue. It is the worst part of night travelling, that it unfits one for much sight-seeing the next day, and thus the time is as much lost as it would be in the train. While Mr. Horner and Tommy went out to find their bankers, Miss Lejeune and Bessie were refreshed with delicious baths, which were to be had in this hotel. The others returned with their hands full of letters from America, England, and Luz, the little place in the Pyréneés where were Mary, Philip and their mother.

"Oh, how splendid!" exclaimed Bessie, as she took her share. "But I am so sleepy that I must go to bed, and read them afterward. Is everybody well, papa?" she asked, for she saw the well-known handwriting of her mother upon the sheet he was reading.

"Perfectly; and they seem very happy there," he answered.

"I must write them volumes," she continued; "but how hard it will be when we want to be in the streets all the time!"

"You had better take long naps, both of you," said Mr. Horner, "and Tommy, too. Almuerzo is eleven, and after that we can drive or walk."

Mr. Horner had letters of introduction to several people in Madrid, but he did not deliver them at this time. It was their plan to come back to Madrid later, after taking their fill of Andalusia, and the southern wonders of Spain.

Nevertheless, they wished to see all they could of the national capital this time, and in the afternoon, thoroughly refreshed by sleep, and almuerzo, and with glowing and grateful hearts, because of good news in all their letters, they took an open carriage to drive about Madrid.

Their driver was a Madrileño, but with the help of a few words of explanation given him by the *portier*, who spoke everything, before starting, they made him understand that they wished to see the principal points of interest within the city.

PUERTA DEL SOL.

The Puerta del Sol, the central square of Madrid, is a large sunny space with a fountain in the middle, wide streets and broad sidewalks surrounding it, and tall handsome buildings on all sides, chiefly hotels with gay shops on the street-floor. There are tracks for the *ferro-carril*, tramway, or horse-cars, as we call them; besides, in Madrid, there are large heavy vehicles like horse-cars, which go where they please; not on any track. The plaza and streets leading from it are so wide that these cars do not encumber them, nor interfere materially with the crowds of gay equipages which throng them, especially on Sunday, when all the world is going to the Bull Ring.

The Horners were not going to the Bull Ring, but their carriage joined the gay crowd sweeping in that direction, along the slope of the Calle de Alcala, passing the Fountain of Cibeles, where they turned to drive along the Prado, a broad, beautiful avenue planted with trees and ornamented with fountains, whose plashing water sparkled in the sun. Iron chairs were placed in rows, which could be hired for a trifling sum, by any one wishing to rest. Here first the Horners observed the "cooling-drinks shops,"—booths where all sorts of refreshing and not intoxicating drinks are sold. The Spanish have an extreme fondness for this harmless refreshment. The number of such places shows the demand for them. The venders call out, "*Agua fresca como la nieve*" (water cool as snow), and for a very small coin they will furnish a glass of something cold and sweet, flavored with strange essences. Tommy's favorite was *horchata de chufas*, a very superior beverage of a milky appearance, and a flavor something like orgeat. All these drinks are very mild, and are but slightly tinged with the flavoring substance. There has to be a good deal of "make-believe," as in the case of the lemonade of the Marchioness, in order to discover what one is tasting. It gives a pleasant impression of the moderation in the taste of a people which contents itself with such mild refreshment, instead of the heavy lager which the German loves, or the fiery drinks of all Northern nations.

The booths where these things are furnished are kept by some old woman, very friendly, offering chairs, or perhaps a small girl, hardly tall enough to reach across her counter. The water used is in tall jars, porous, to keep the water cool by perspiration, a thing the Horners had learned to understand on the Nile.

It was much later that the children became learned in cooling

COOLING DRINKS.

drinks. On that first day they only wondered at the little stalls where they were sold.

There were so many things to see that they could not fasten their attention upon any one set of impressions. Their heads were turning from side to side, to catch glimpses of fine horses dashing by them; — ladies in full costume, mantilla and fan, leaning back in their open carriages, — fountains, monuments, fine buildings, set their brains in a whirl.

Madrid is said to have little or nothing Spanish about it; to be a feeble imitation of Paris; in short, only a second-rate European metropolis. The Horners did not agree with this verdict, for they found it marked, on the contrary, with great individuality. The streets and modern buildings are after the manner of French models, undoubtedly, but there is a Southern swing in the life and movement of the sun-bathed city; and though the population has a European character in its dress, many picturesque costumes are to be seen. The equipages and horses exhibit an amount of

EL BUEN RETIRO.

wealth, taste and extravagance at least equal to that of any city of the same size in Europe.

They passed the façade of the Royal Museum, which contains the famous picture gallery, promising themselves, on their return from Andalusia, many visits to its treasures. It is a modern building with columns, imposing in appearance, though perhaps too low for its great length. It was fitted up for pictures in the early part of this century; the collection of splendid works of art it contains makes it perhaps the finest gallery in the world.

They drove through the Buen Retiro, a pleasant shady promenade planted with hedges of lilac and other spring flowers, still in bloom. Their driver brought them back by a turn quite around the town, that they might see the outside of the handsome Royal Palace, and through the Plaza del Oriente, where is a fine equestrian statue of Philip the Fourth on his war charger. The design was by Velasquez, and Galileo is said to have suggested the means by which the balance is preserved. The horse is rearing so high that this is affected only by having the front part hollow, and the back solid.

CHAPTER VIII.

HISTORICAL.

AS they were coming back to their hotel through the steep and somewhat narrow Calle Mayor, a train of royal carriages passed them. At first, Bessie and Tommy thought they were to meet his Majesty face to face, but it was only the royal baby returning from her airing, in two carriages, with postilions and outriders. The poor little thing, although wrapped about in rich robes of soft white, looked as helpless as any other mortal child. She is an object for sympathy rather than envy, because she is a princess, when she should have been a prince, heir to the throne upon which her papa finds his seat somewhat unsteady.

It is now nine years since Alphonso the Twelfth was proclaimed king at Madrid. He is the eldest son of Isabella the Second, herself the daughter of King Ferdinand the Seventh, and of Princess Marie Christine of the two Sicilies. Isabella was proclaimed queen in 1833, when she was but three years old. Ten years later, when she was thirteen, she was declared to be of age by a decree of the Cortes, and was married not long after to her first cousin, Francisco, a son of the brother of King Ferdinand the Seventh. It might seem that the eldest son of parents, both of whom have a claim to the throne, would have made his way to it, without opposition, in the due course of events; but this has not been the case. On the contrary, civil war raged from the time of Isabella's accession to the throne up to the moment when her son was placed upon it, and ever since politicians and patriots have watched with anxiety the doubtful experiment of a government under the present constitution,— a monarchy shorn of the splendors which formerly added so much to the presence of a king, and closely restricted in its powers.

The constitution declares Alphonso the Twelfth of Bourbon, to be the legitimate king of Spain. His person is inviolable, but his ministers are responsible, and all his orders must be countersigned by a minister. There is a Cortes, which shares the power of the king,

FOUNTAIN OF NEPTUNE.

composed, like our Congress, of two legislative bodies. The Senate is composed of sons of kings and other personages, and the Congress of Deputies chosen by the people.

Thus it will be seen, that the plan is to have the government as free as that of a Republic, while the head of it is called a king, and he is permitted to be the head on account of his hereditary rights, instead of being the choice of the people; yet he would not remain at the head for an instant without the assent of the public. A country which from all time has been governed by kings, probably feels more at ease under the nominal rule of a monarch; and this is the present condition of things in Spain. Repuplican government has been tried more than once in the tempestuous period since the death of Ferdinand, in 1833; and it is because all lovers of Spanish prosperity feel that the only hope for Spain is in a period of peace and tranquility, that there is a general hope for a continuance of the experiment by which Alphonso and his dynasty may be firmly established upon the throne. For this reason, a little prince would be hailed with delight as heir to the throne. The Spaniards would be kindled to something like enthusiasm for a future king, born in a peaceful period, of the line of inherited royalty; so the disappointment was great when a little princess appeared into the world. She should have been a prince, and this is why the Horners called her the poor little princess, in spite of her having a duchess for governess, and outriders before and behind when she takes her little airing.

"How stupid of her not to be a prince!" said Tommy, when these things were being explained to him.

"She cannot help it," said Bessie, "and it is a shame that people should not be just as fond of her as fifty boys."

"I dare say her papa and mamma are fond of her," said Miss Lejeune; "it is only the public that is disappointed. Very likely she will have a much happier life than a little prince would have done. In the first place she will not be spoiled," —

"Nor fussed over about her health," continued Bessie, "nor made to wear crowns and carry sceptres. I dare say she will live to a peaceful old age, with plenty to eat and drink, and good clothes, in a comfortable palace all her life."

"And paint very nicely in water-colors," added Miss Lejeune.

It is perhaps necessary to touch briefly upon the troubles in Spain which have brought the nation to this fervent desire for peace and repose on any terms.

Ferdinand the Seventh was an unworthy, contemptible king; one of the worst specimens of the Bourbon type. His father, Charles the Fourth, abdicated the throne in terror, the nineteenth of March, 1808, when Napoleon's army was marching upon Madrid, and announced his son Ferdinand as his successor; whom, too, Napoleon forced to abdicate, for as usual, it was his plan to furnish his own king to

Spain; and Joseph Bonaparte entered Madrid and took possession of the throne. But this could not be allowed to last. The opposition of the Spaniards was enforced by the arrival of ten thousand English troops in Portugal, under Sir Arthur Wellesley, who now for the first time began that resistance to Napoleon which, as Wellington, he crowned at Waterloo. The struggle in Spain lasted six years, but by that time the invincible legions of Napoleon were defeated. During this time the Emperor himself descended upon Madrid; Sir John Moore was defeated and killed, the wonderful siege of Saragossa took place, when the resisting Spaniards, conducted by Palafox, and inspired by the maid of Saragossa, held out fifty days against the French, and many another disaster fell upon one army or the other; but in the end the French were driven out, and left the country after the famous battle of Vittoria, June, 1813, when Wellington, as Sir Arthur Wellesley had already become, ended the contest.

FERDINAND VII.

Joseph was deposed, Ferdinand was reinstated. At the same time another Bourbon prince, Louis the Eighteenth returned to rule in France, for Napoleon's career was over.

But a worthless prince, like Ferdinand, had no power, if he had inclination, to heal the wounds of a country bleeding after the contest of six years. Civil war broke out, and with it came misery, famine and ruin. Ferdinand was carried off to Cadiz a prisoner by his subjects, but was again liberated by a foreign army, this time from France. It was after this that he married his fourth wife, Maria Christina, 1829, his own niece. In 1830, their daughter Isabella was born. It will not now appear surprising that this princess was not at the time regarded with much affection. Her chance of reigning was but slight, although at her birth the law allowed women to succeed; but it was comparatively modern, and all Spanish prejudice was, and is, in favor of the Salic law, by which a woman can reign only in default of male heirs. Now the king had a brother whose claim was fairly good to the throne; who moreover had sons in plenty to furnish heirs, one of whom, Don Carlos, born in 1788, had an absolute right to the throne in default of male heirs.

This is the foundation of the so-called Carlist War, which lasted up to the time of Alphonso's arrival upon the throne. Ferdinand died shortly after the birth of Isabella, but her mother, Christina, was very popular as regent, and in her name the contest was carried on.

CHRISTINA.

During this time the state of the country was so unsettled that travelling was almost impossible. Lawlessness prevailed, brigands were free to attack and carry off people they met, and hold them for treason. All internal improvements were at a standstill, and high-roads and railways were far behind the general standard of Europe.

All this has greatly changed for the better, and tourists, even if indifferent to the welfare of the Spanish race, must be grateful to the present state of order which renders travelling as easy and comfortable as in any part of Europe, making allowance for certain drawbacks made inevitable by long distances.

The Carlist contest, after many successes and defeats, came to an end in 1840. Isabella the Second came herself to the throne, and there was again hope of repose for the country; but she was quite unworthy to govern, being incapable of governing herself; a series of ministers held the affairs of state. Although some of them were of the first order of capacity to deal well with difficult matters, there came a time when Isabella was driven from the throne into exile; a provisional government was formed, and every plan was suggested for a permanent one; and finally a new king was elected, by the Cortes, the Duke of Aosta, Amadeo, son of Victor Emmanuel.

ISABELLA II.

He was invested with the royal dignities on the second of January, 1871; but not later than February, 1873, he abdicated, having found it impossible to govern constitutionally in Spain; his life had been attempted, his queen was rudely treated by the grand Spanish ladies, and he was conspicuously unpopular with the people. Thus was shown the strange spectacle of the throne of Spain, which was once the seat of the greatest power, and also the centre of the splendor of the world, abandoned voluntarily by the occupant chosen for it!

Then came what was called republican government. Almost any one who was willing to try his hand at playing President might have a chance. The reaction from this chaotic state of things brought about the coming of the present king, a thoroughly educated prince, brought up far away from his ignoble mother, in France and England.

His life has been a sad one in one respect. He was first married to his cousin Mercedes, the daughter of the Duke of Montpensier, a young lady said by all to have been sweet and lovely, and sincerely loved by her husband. She died, and he is now married to an Austrian princess, Maria Christina, who is the mother of the little girl the Horners saw, and of another princess who was born afterwards, in the summer of 1882.

It has been for those who have lived through the period we have just been touching upon, so confusing to follow in brief newspaper bulletins the ups and downs of the Spanish peninsula, that some outsiders are, like the Horners, but ill-informed upon the subject. As they were now in the country, they found it interesting as well as desirable to study up the subject, and the result of their researches is what is here given.

THE VEGETABLE DEALER.

CHAPTER IX.

AN INCIDENT.

COAT OF ARMS OF TOLEDO.

JUST as the Horners drove up to the door of the hotel, through the plaza crowded with people, they had the luck to see the king and all his suite, driving by on their return from the bull-fight. The bull-fight was late, the king was late, worst of all the Horners were late, and the *table d'hote* dinner nearly over when they entered the dining-room: only a few people were lingering over dessert, or sipping their coffee. The patient, assiduous waiters, however, cheerfully prepared to begin all over again. They showed them to their seats, brought the soup, and resigned themselves to bringing back all the courses of the long dinner.

"It is really too bad we are so late," said Miss Lejeune. "I am always sorry for the waiters."

"It is a pity, but they are used to it," said Mr. Horner; "besides, we could not help it, for the streets were so blocked our driver had to go slowly."

"We did not see the king coming back, after all," said Tommy. Just as he was speaking, a waiter who flattered himself he spoke English, said:

"Look you now here, my master, they come!"

And sure enough, the whole royal procession swept by, outriders, carriages, and the long train of escorts, in handsome uniforms, with white burnous thrown on their shoulders, more gorgeous than their simple morning-array.

"This is doing pretty well, Tommy, to see the king twice on your first day in Madrid!" said his father.

They went back to their dinner, and devoted themselves to it, for they all were hungry, and it was very good. As it went on, Bessie and Tommy began to take notice of a party lower down the table, who were having, not a regular dinner, but a sort of supper. A French nurse was superintending the group, which consisted of a boy about Tommy's age, a little girl somewhat younger, and a fat and chubby child which brandished arms and legs in the crude manner belonging to the age of three years or less.

They had bowls of milk, and were eating bread and butter and orange marmalade, and talking both French and English with their mouths full.

"I say, Nana," said the boy, "you might have taken us to the bull-fight. That gentleman said at breakfast that it was the noblest sight in the world."

The nurse replied in French, though she understood his English:

"I cannot take you to bull courses. When your papa comes he can do so, if he sees fit."

"When papa comes!" the boy exclaimed impatiently. "You are always saying that. I do not believe he ever will come!"

"Of course he will come, Hubert!" said the little girl, who had rather a high voice, but a clear-cut English way of speaking. "We have only been two days in Madrid, and he does not know yet."

"But I wanted him to be here when we arrived," he replied. "It is all very well for you girls to be mewed up with Nana, but I need the companionship of a man."

Bessie and Tommy glanced at each other with signs of amusement, when the English boy made this speech Just then the little child, while Nana was looking the other way, made a clutch at a dish of oranges just out of reach. She lost her balance, having, in fact, a somewhat insecure seat upon cushions put in a common chair to make it high enough. In falling, she grasped the tablecloth, and pulled it far enough to overturn the oranges, and to set glasses, finger-

BRIDGE OF SAINT MARTIN, TOLEDO.

bowls, knives and forks sliding about. Nana turned at once; but Tommy, who was nearest the party, sprang first to the rescue, and picked up the baby almost before her head touched the ground. Of course she was frightened, however, and screamed. The English children tried to steady the sliding tablecloth; the waiters, who had

HOSPITAL OF SANTA CRUZ, EARLY 16TH CENTURY.

all retired from the scene, hurried back. The commotion was over in a few minutes, and nothing serious had happened; a wineglass had broken in falling to the ground, and a good deal of water was spilt; but that was all.

The incident served as the beginning of an acquaintance, for not only Bessie and Tommy, but Mr. Horner and Miss Lejeune, left their dinner to help the nurse to restore order, and to console the children who were dismayed.

Miss Lejeune took a napkin and dried the front of the elder girl's dress, while Nana carried off the screaming baby, saying as she went, to the other children, rather crossly, "Come up, now, and go to bed. This is enough trouble for one day."

"Go to bed!" said Hubert. "Not I. I shall go out and walk in the Puerta del Sol."

Seeing the children thus left to themselves, Mr. Horner ventured to ask them if they were alone.

"Why, yes, all but Nana!" Hubert explained. "We are on the way to Gibraltar, and we left mamma at Bordeaux to go up in the Pyrénées. And papa was to meet us here, but we arrived first, and there is no letter. So Nana says we must wait, which is all very well for girls, but she does not let me go anywhere!"

"You promised mamma, Hubert," said his sister fretfully, "that you would take care of Nana, and me, and baby."

"Yes; but I did not promise to go to bed before dark!"

The boy was evidently chafed by too much petticoat government. Tommy pitied him, and Mr. Horner was not surprised at his impatience.

"I'll tell you what you shall do," said Miss Lejeune. "Fanny,— is not your name Fanny?" she paused to ask.

The little girl nodded assent.

"Run and tell Nana that we have invited you both to spend the evening with us. You can say that Mr. Horner is an American gentleman travelling through Spain;—she will be sure to let you come. Then she can put the baby to bed, and rest herself. I do not know what we shall do, but there is plenty to see from our windows.

Hubert's brow cleared. He put on a manly air and bowed very politely, thanking them all for their kindness, and told Fanny to take the message.

"My father, Colonel Vaughan, will thank you when he comes," he added.

Bessie went with her to show her afterwards the way to their room, to which they all adjourned. A box of sugar plums which Tommy had bought in the morning, served to promote ease and hilarity. The children were soon talking together freely in the balcony, and Miss Lejeune and Mr. Horner settled themselves at the round table to write.

"I wonder who they are," said Miss Lejeune in a low voice when she was quite sure the children would not overhear her. "It seems strange that they should be alone with the nurse."

"The father is very likely stationed at Gibraltar," said Mr. Horner. "Hubert called him *Colonel* Vaughan, you know. It seems rather a loose way to look after his children to send them across Spain with nobody but a French woman to look after them."

"There must be some special reason for it," said Miss Lejeune. "I wonder they did not take a steamer round to Gibraltar."

"We shall learn more about it, I dare say," said Mr. Horner; "meanwhile I am glad we can amuse them for this one evening. I am sorry we must leave them to-morrow. By the way, Augusta," — and here Mr. Horner interrupted himself to look for the guide-books and time-tables,— "I have an idea!"

"What is it?" asked Miss Augusta with a smile.

"It is that we should go to Toledo now, instead of waiting till we come back from Granada. The season is so backward that I have no fear of the heat at the South, have you?"

"Not the least," she replied. "It is a very good plan, for we shall then have Toledo off our minds when we come back. What gave you this good idea?"

"It was thinking of the Goths, you see," said Mr. Horner, laughing, "when it occurred to me that it would be better to study their great capital before going down among the Moors."

"Well, well! you are improving," cried Miss Lejeune. "For a man who said last week that he had even no knowledge of the map of Spain, to now show that he knows the difference between Goths and Moors! Evidently you have been read-ing up!" she added with a smile.

"Not only have I been reading up," he returned, "but I have been talking with one of the gentle-men at the bank. He says that Toledo is perfectly wonder-ful, and that we ought to devote sev-eral days to it, and moreover, he has given me the ad-dress of a sort of *pension* to go to instead of the hotel."

"Very well," said Miss Lejeune, "and how about trains?" she continued.

"That is what we must now look up." They busied them-selves on the subject, and after half an hour of careful study, had arranged a plan.

ZOCODOVER IN TOLEDO.

"Children," said Miss Augusta, advancing to the window where the new acquaintances were "getting on splendidly," as they would have expressed it, "we are going to Toledo to-morrow."

"Toledo!" cried Bessie, "I thought"—

"We have changed the plan," said her father.

"Oh!" she exclaimed; "then I must go at once and read about the Goths!" and she jumped into the room.

"I wish *we* could go to Toledo," said Hubert mournfully, reverting to his lonely position which these new companions had made him for a while forget.

"What are your plans?" asked Mr. Horner kindly; "perhaps I can advise you."

"We are just waiting here, sir," he replied, "for a letter, or some message from papa, telling us how to go on. I dare say he has sent it, but Spanish mails are so slow." Then, as if he thought Mr. Horner might be wondering why they were stranded at Madrid in this manner, he added, while the color came into his cheeks, "We are going to papa, because my mother was too ill to keep us with her, and she thought,— she thought I was old enough to bring them as far as here. But it is too hard,— it is too hard to have to wait;" and after a struggle, he broke down, and burst into sobs, with his head on his arm, leaning upon the balcony railing in the dark.

"It is hard for you, my dear boy," said Mr. Horner, putting his arm kindly round his shoulder, "and I am glad we met you, because I am sure we can help you. We will see to-morrow about telegraphing to your father, if no letter comes."

CHAPTER X.

THE VAUGHANS.

NEXT morning Miss Lejeune had a little talk with Nana, the French nurse of the Vaughan children, who proved to be an intelligent and faithful woman, fit to be entrusted with the sole charge of them, on ordinary occasions. She was doing her best, but the unexpected failure to meet Colonel Vaughan made her task more difficult than had been intended. She was very grateful for the interest which Miss Lejeune readily showed, and thankful for advice as to her course.

"You see, madam," she said, "the children were to have stayed with their mother during the summer, but madam became so very ill the doctor said they must be taken from her. Her disease is of the nerves. Poor lady! she is very delicate. We wrote to Gibraltar, and had one letter from the father, and were told to come here. It was not so very difficult by the train. We left my lady at Pau."

"And you have no letter since?" asked Miss Lejeune.

"No letter," replied the nurse. "Mr. Hubert goes daily to the banker's, but there is nothing, and he is growing very impatient."

Meanwhile Mr. Horner took both the boys out with him, and as soon as it was late enough for the bank to be open, they went there; it was the same place for their own letters and for Hubert's.

"This is the third time I have been here, and always the same answer, 'Nothing for you, sir,'" said Hubert, as they climbed the stairs; "but you will bring me luck, I hope," he added, smiling.

Mr. Horner liked the boy. His smile was bright, and the look which came from his eyes frank and direct. He was slightly built.

and decidedly smaller than Tommy, who was now a stout, strong lad, promising soon to be as tall as his brother Philip.

They went into the banking office, and two or three clerks looked up at their entrance, one of whom rose to meet Mr. Horner with a bow.

"Mr. Agrazis has not come in, sir; can we do anything for you?"

"Yes;" replied Mr. Horner. "I hardly expect any letters myself to-day, but I hope you will find one for this young gentleman."

The clerk turned to another, who seemed to have the charge of customers' letters, and they exchanged several words in Spanish.

"I know perfectly well," said Hubert to Tommy, "that they are saying to each other. 'There is that everlasting boy bothering us about his letters.' They are just determined I shall not have any."

"No, sir; nothing at all," said the clerk, running through a bunch of decrepit old letters which looked as if they had been in stock since the flood. He took them out of a pigeon-hole in a set like that in a country post-office, marked with the letters of the alphabet.

"Pardon me," said Mr. Horner, "may I look for myself?" He took the bunch, then said, "This is not the right bundle; Vaughan begins with V."

"Faun, Faun," repeated the Spanish clerk; "ah, no?"

They all looked for themselves into pigeon-hole V., and there the solitary letter was lying, a blue envelope directed in a clear, bold hand, to

MASTER HUBERT VAUGHAN
Care of Messrs. Agrazis and Brown
Banqueros, Madrid

Hubert pounced on it, too glad to find it to resent the mistake, but Mr. Horner could not help mildly asking the clerk how long it had probably been there.

"Oh! last night, last night only. Very positive," he replied; and

SANTA MARIA LA BIANCA

Mr. Horner would not press the matter. Hubert was tearing open the letter, and soon had mastered its contents. It was dated at the very earliest moment that Colonel Vaughan had news of the plan of sending the children to him by the way of Madrid. It had probably been lying in the pigeon-hole at the bank as long as the Vaughans had been waiting for it; but this did not much signify, as the contents proved. It was brief, and ran thus:

Dear Hubert:
You will find this on your arrival at Madrid. I am very sorry that you are obliged to come, but will do my best to meet you, or send some one, before the end of the month. You will stay, of course, at the Hotel de la Paix, where I am perfectly well known. Be a good boy and mind Nana.
Your Affectionate Father,
James Vaughan.

Mr. Horner and Tommy stood waiting while Hubert read his letter, which to be sure did not take long. Mr. Horner saw at a glance that he was disappointed and hurt. He hesitated, began to put the letter in his pocket, squeezing his lips tightly together; then changing his mind, handed it up to Mr. Horner, with a helpless movement, as if he surrendered himself, in that movement, to the guardianship of his new friend.

"The end of the month!" he said in a low voice, as if he meant the end of the world. It was now only the sixteenth.

Tommy took the liberty of looking over his father's shoulder. He thought it was an unkind letter; and, to tell the truth, Mr. Horner formed no glowing impression of Colonel Vaughan from reading it; but it was too early to judge his character. He handed it back, saying briefly:

"Come along, boys; we will go and see what Nana says. Good morning, gentlemen. Tommy, your umbrella!" And they all went down into St. Geronimo street, through which they must pass to their hotel. The street looked changed, to them, though it was as lively as ever, thronged with well-dressed men, women with mantillas, dogs, donkey-carts, carriages, hand-organs; the shop windows were as gay, and the gaudy fan which Bessie longed for was flaunting just as brightly as when they had stopped to look at it the day before, but Madrid had become hateful to Hubert, and Tommy was very angry with the unknown father of his new friend, who could write such a letter as that.

"The end of the month," repeated Mr. Horner; then he asked abruptly, "Hubert, should you like to go with us to Toledo?"

"To Toledo! Could you take me? O, Mr. Horner!"

"Papa!" exclaimed Tommy, "oh, do let him go!"

"Let us see what Nana thinks," said Mr. Horner, whereat the two boys started for the hotel on the full run across the crowded plaza, finding their way with great skill between the legs of the horses. Just at the door, they all came luckily upon Miss Lejeune and Bessie, who were setting forth by themselves for a little stroll.

EMPTY WINE JARS.

"Where is Nana? Do you know?"

"She is up there at the balcony of the salon," said Bessie, pointing with her parasol. "She wanted Fanny to stay and help take care of the baby."

The matter was arranged sooner and more simply than Mr. Horner had expected; for it seemed that the head waiter of the Hotel de la Paix was the husband of Nana's sister, so that Nana was perfectly at home in the hotel, where she had once or twice before accompanied her mistress, Mrs. Vaughan.

She thought it perfectly proper for Mr. Horner to take Hubert and Fanny, who was of course included in the scheme, to Toledo for a few days, while she stayed in the hotel at Madrid looking after the baby. When she heard of the letter from Colonel Vaughan, she shook her head and said:

SIX-MULE TEAM, TOLEDO.

"I thought as much. Very likely it will be the end of another month. He is in no hurry, madam," she added, turning to Miss Lejeune with a knowing nod, but a smile of sadness, "to take charge of the children."

But the children did not hear this. They had scampered off to get ready for Toledo. Mr. Horner called after them:

"Put up things enough for three days, Hubert!"

"*Mon Dieu! mon Dieu!*" cried Nana, catching up the baby and running after them; "with all the *linge* at the *blanchisseuse*, shall there be even a *mouchoir* between them!"

As the *blanchisseuse* was the very sister who had married the head waiter, this matter was arranged without delay.

"Well!" said Miss Lejeune to Mr. Horner, when they were left alone in the little balcony.

"Well!" returned Mr. Horner, "this is a pretty high-handed proceeding!"

"How exactly like you," said Miss Lejeune, "to take these wandering children wholly upon trust, and carry them off with you!"

"As for that, I am not afraid the children will pick our pockets, or put poison in the soup; but if the stern parent should change his mind and come after them" —

"And find the birds flown," said Miss Lejeune, continuing his thought, "it might be a little awkward. But Nana would be equal to the occasion. Besides, he will not come. What a letter!"

"I am most anxious about Nana; what if she neglects the baby in our absence?" said Mr. Horner.

"My dear, we are not responsible for that baby. Suppose we had never met them, it would be just the same."

"In taking the children, we assume the burden of the whole family, I believe," said Mr. Horner, shaking his head. While they were talking, they had returned to their apartment. Mr. Horner was walking up and down the room, with his hands in his pockets. He went on to say:

"It is a risk, but I think it will turn out well. I shall set Hubert to writing to his father at once, before we leave for Toledo, and I shall add a postscript, to make it all right with Colonel Vaughan. So now, we must make all ready for the start this afternoon. Have you much to do?"

"No," replied Miss Lejuene; "as we only take the little things, and leave the trunks here. But you had better send Bessie to me if you see her."

He left the room. When Miss Lejeune was alone, she exclaimed aloud, "Was there ever"— finishing her thought inwardly thus: "a man so enlarged and improved as Philip Horner, by marriage and the intercourse with intelligent women! Twenty years ago, he would not have taken so much trouble for his own relations, and here he is going out of his way to give pleasure to some little stray children. And he born in Boston!"

CHAPTER XI.

CALLE ISABEL, 16.

BRIDGE OF ALCANTARA.

THUS Nana was left with the baby, and the young Vaughans, amazed and delighted, joined the Horners for Toledo. Little Fanny was shy, and wanted at first to be left with Nana. Less notice had been taken of her than of her brother, and she had not the same adaptability that he possessed; still it seemed a pity to leave her behind, and though Bessie did not care much about the child yet, she exerted herself to urge her going.

They reached Toledo after dark, and found at the station an omnibus with mules, like the one at Burgos, only this time the drive to the town was longer, and the mules were even more animated. There were eight of them, and they whirled along at a mad pace, the driver cracking his whip, and the postilion running at the side, or jumping up on the front animal, who was a horse, by the way, and not a mule.

Toledo is built on a high rock, almost perpendicular on all sides but one. It is seen from a great distance above the plain, with sombre stone buildings rising in terraces one above the other. The Tagus winds its way beneath the walls in a sort of horseshoe, through a deep bed with steep, cañon-like sides. They crossed it by the bridge of Alcantara — or Al Kantarah, which means a bridge in Arabic — passing under arches and through towers at either end, and then they began slowly winding up through the town. It had been light enough to see the river and the bridge, but darkness came on soon, and they could not tell where they were. The streets were so narrow that they were close to the windows of shops which seemed brilliant in the dimly-lighted streets, and could see all sorts of Spanish things, tinsel church ornaments, bright silk or cotton handkerchiefs, and brass work. The omnibus was feebly lighted by a dim oil lamp, but Bessie managed to make out that the only person besides themselves in it, who sat in the corner by the door, was a matador in his bull-fight dress. He had his little spadas, or swords, with him, under the seat.

"This is the best fun of anything yet in Spain!" cried Tommy

DONKEYS CARRYING WATER JARS.

joyously, between the bumps of the swaying vehicle, and Hubert, who had come direct from Bayonne to Madrid in the train without stopping, fully agreed with him.

They stopped before a large wooden door, which reminded them of an Eastern Bab, or gate. An unseen cord pulled it open, and it swung inward, showing by the light of a candle, in a small niche in a thick wall, a broad flight of stairs, built, as far as they could

LOOKING BACK ACROSS THE BRIDGE.

make out, on one side of an open court, or *patio*. They groped their way up two sets of stairs, and there were met by two elderly Spanish señoras with hospitable manners, like any two ladies awaiting to receive their guests. The Horners had been prepared for this, and had got together their best Spanish; and it now came out, what they had not before thought of, that Hubert, who had spent most of his life in Gibraltar, could manage the language pretty well.

These sweet ladies made them welcome, and led them by a corridor running round the patio, to a huge room, with small windows, heavy beams running across the ceiling, and in one corner an ancient, closed-up door of green corroded iron, through which Bessie fancied that Roderick the Goth might step into the room at any moment. There were two little iron beds against the wall, and there was room in the great chamber for half a dozen more. The two girls, with Miss Lejeune, were put in possession, while the señoras carried of the others. Philip and his father were given a room whose one window opened upon the corridor, and Hubert's room was a little dark place leading from this up three steps, with a big flowered chintz curtain for a door or portière.

While one señora bustled about making them comfortable, the other disappeared to superintend their supper. The ladies were soon restored by fresh water, which was brought in hospitable profusion, and while Miss Lejeune rested on the bed, the girls leaned upon the window and looked down into the patio. It was a square window, with folding sashes, and heavy shutters, all painted a faded green. Below, through the darkness, they could make out a paved square court with oleander-trees in green boxes, and in mysterious corners stood huge jars which might have contained a forty-thief apiece. A bell rang which they recognized by the sound, as the door-bell their driver had rung when they came; and then a wonderful thing happened. The señora, who had been bringing them water and towels, appeared at a window of the corridor, just opposite the one where the children were standing, and pulled at a cord. They could not see round the corner down below, but they knew that she must have opened the front door by this process, from the conversation which ensued in Spanish. Of course they could not understand it, but they guessed, and probably were nearly right, that it was something like this:

The señora said, "Well! who's there?"

"It is Pepe, señora. The butterman has no butter."

"What! Then you must run to the milkman."

"I have done so, and he has none."

PUERTA DEL SOL, TOLEDO.

"Fetch me, then, some fresh oil, for we have but little; but be quick, for the strangers are already impatient for their supper."

The invisible messenger said no more. As the señora loosened the rope, the great door swung to with a bang.

Soon the bell rang again, and the same process took place. This time there was a scuffling below, and the shadowy form of Pepe was to be seen hurrying up the stairs which led from the patio below, in full view of the children's post of observation.

Over their heads the stars were shining brightly against the clear evening sky; pointed dormer windows in the tiled roof which went around the four sides of the patio, stood out sharply; every now and then a little bird, which speaks often at night in Spain, made its plaintive note close at hand. It was wonderfully still and strange.

Still they were not sorry to be summoned to supper, which was served to them alone, at a round table lighted by a swinging lamp. The kind ladies waited on them, and watched to see if they liked the good chicken and fried eggs which they provided. The Horners praised everything, to the graceful brown jug that held the water. Little Fanny, too tired and sleepy to eat much, was an object of great interest to the hostesses, and one of them offered to put her to bed before the rest had finished their apricots; but Miss Lejeune would not allow this.

She was afraid Fanny might be frightened in the great room with the green iron door; but she was a passive little traveller, and in fact fell asleep as soon as her head was on the pillow.

"I hope Roderick the Goth will not come in and terrify her," said Miss Lejeune, as she resumed her seat at the table, and began to sip the black coffee, which, late as it was, she had not feared to accept.

"Who is Roderick the Goth?" demanded Hubert; "you keep referring to him."

"He was the last of the Goths, so called," said Miss Lejeune, "but we use his name because he was a famous one, and we have the Goths upon our minds, because during their rule in Spain,

Toledo was their chief place; and while we are here, we expect to see the traces of their buildings and ways of doing things."

"I do not know anything about history," said Hubert with a tone partly scornful and partly meek, if such a combination can be possible.

"Well, you see, *you* are in Spain because you have to be," said Tommy; "but as we are here for fun, we want to get all the fun we can out of a country, by knowing all we can about it."

"Bravo, Tommy!" exclaimed his father; "these are the true Horner sentiments."

"Well, then, you will have to tell me all you know," said Hubert, "for I am rather late to begin."

"Now, I will tell you very briefly," said Bessie, "the way I used to tell Phil, if you will only listen."

"I think, Bessie, your general glimpse of the Goths had better be postponed," said Mr. Horner, "for it is long after ten o'clock, and we ought all to go to bed."

"All right," said Hubert, who was struggling with a great yawn, "but I will listen to-morrow, Bessie."

The early chroniclers of Toledo say that the city was founded at least as far back as the creation of the world; without trying to verify their theories, it is quite probable that the Romans found something there when they established themselves as early as the beginning of the third century, A. D. At all events, it was to the Romans an important centre. The first council of the Church of Spain was held at Toledo, 400 A. D. Some time later, upon the irruption of the barbarians of the North, which swept all over the peninsula, it became the capital of Gothic Spain, and was very prosperous and important. In Wamba's reign, the glory of Toledo reached its climax; but from that time the Gothic name began to decline through its own corruption and internal quarrels, all of which were preparing for the downfall of the monarchy. Secret intelligence was given to the Moors over in Africa, that there was a chance for successful invasion, and they landed at Gibraltar in great numbers.

Roderick, with all his Goths, came out to meet them, and a great battle was fought, not far from Cadiz, on the banks of the Guadelete. Roderick advanced towards the enemy, dressed in gold and purple, standing in his ivory chariot, with a wonderful headdress, and two mules splendidly accoutred. These signs of royalty made him an easy mark, and he was cut down by the weapon of the Turk. The head of the king was cut off and forwarded to the court of Damascus. Thus fell the monarchy of the Goths, and thus began the domination of the Moor, whose rule in Spain lasted eight hundred years. They, too, at first, made Toledo their chief place until Cordova became their court and capital.

CHAPTER XII.

TOLEDO.

DURING all the centuries, the great races who have appeared in Spain, lived their life, and vanished, have had some foothold in Toledo. They have all left their traces there, which are yet to be seen, although the city has now become a place of little importance other than its many monuments of the past. Old Roman archways, the traces of the palace of the Gothic kings, beautiful specimens of Moorish mosques and of Jewish synagogues, are still visible; for when Toledo was first taken by the Moors it was filled with Hebrews, who helped the Moors because they had been persecuted by their previous rulers, the Goths. The Cathedral, and the Church of San Juan de los Reyes, are monuments of the Spanish Christians, and the present century is represented by the destruction wrought by French soldiers in 1810.

The streets are irregular, ill-paved, and steep and winding; but this intricacy was intentional, for it made them easy to defend when attacked, and kept them cool in summer. The houses are for the most part Moorish, built about patios, or courts, over which awnings are drawn in summer.

In the heart of the city towers the Cathedral, around which cluster many churches and convents, now silent and deserted. The silence of the place strikes the ear at once, where no carriages, and but seldom a footfall, disturb the echoes of the narrow streets.

The Horners passed three delightful days there, going back to Madrid on the evening of the third. The hospitable sisters, who kept the house, would fain have them stay a month, and they were so enchanted with their quarters, nothing would have pleased them better.

PROCESSION OF MONKS.

"If Mary were only here!" was Miss Lejeune's exclamation; "there is sketching enough for weeks!"

When the señoras learned just how long they could stay, they planned for them the arrangement of their time, so that they should see as many as possible of the interesting places, and without doing too much at a time, so as to be tired, and lose the impression.

Their first excursion was to walk round the picturesque old city, going down to the Puerta del Sol, not like that of Madrid, changed to mean a broad square, but really a Moorish gate of granite horseshoe arches; and thence along an old road to another gate, where there are outworks built by Wamba the Goth, the new Puerta visagra being the work of Philip the Second. Here, there is an image of St. Eugenio, Bishop of Toledo, who came from France. Going back there he was murdered at St. Denis, and his body remained there until another French bishop discovered it and brought back the right arm to Spain. Philip the Second obtained the rest from Charles the Ninth, and thus all the parts of the sacred remains were reunited at Toledo, after a thousand years of separation, according to the explanation of the guide who went with them to point out the items of interest. It seemed as if there was something to see at every step, and after two or three hours, their heads were turning with the difficulty of following his Spanish explanation. Goths and Moors were growing hopelessly mixed in their minds. The cobblestone pavements tired their feet, and they were hungry, for this was an early start after coffee and before almuerzo. So they insisted upon going back to the Calle St. Isabel, No. 16, to the dismay of the worthy man, who had but just got going on his tour of inspection. They promised to start again after a rest, in the afternoon, and came back after admiring the remains of the Palace Castle, built by Wamba in 674, and the bridge of San Martin, which there completes the picture. This bridge is quite at the opposite curve of the horseshoe made by the Tagus, from the one over which they had entered the city.

In the afternoon, to please the guide, they came back to this point, to inspect the remains of the Franciscan convent, called San

Juan de los Reyes — of the Kings — because it was dedicated by Ferdinand and Isabella to their particular saint, John, being erected by them in 1476, to commemorate a victory over the king of Portugal. The detail of this church is very elaborate, and it is a specimen of the richest Gothic of the Moorish period, although the severest critics condemn the taste of the ornaments, such as the angels with coats of arms, that crowd the walls. On the outside, in one part of the wall, still hang the rusty chains with which Christians were confined by the Moors, won back at the conquest of Grenada. It is said that Ferdinand and Isabella intended to be buried here, but they changed their idea, and their tombs are in the Cathedral at Grenada.

Bessie and Miss Lejeune liked best the old cloister of this church; though it is falling down through neglect and bad usage, it is the finest portion of the whole work, covered with rich sculptures of foliage, and animals and saints, in niches. It was much damaged by French soldiers during the early part of this century, and is now used in part as a picture gallery. The pictures are sad and gloomy, like those in most inferior Spanish collections; and there are no specimens of the best. The courtyard of the cloister was overgrown with tall rose-trees, oleander and other shrubs, whose long neglected sprays twisted about the broken carvings.

During their absence, the good landladies had been engaged in a very serious work, which had occupied their whole day. The Horners found them busily engaged upon it when they came in to almuerzo, but by dinner time all traces of it were removed, and the thing was complete. This was patching and mending the huge awning of the patio, large enough to stretch all over it, across from one side of the roof to another, each way. Early in the morning it was lowered into the court, and there spread out on the flat stone pavement, an odd sight, for the original brownish color was already varied by patches of white, where it had been strengthened from time to time, so that it looked like an immense patchwork quilt of varied shades of yellow, white, and brown.

THE CATHEDRAL OF TOLEDO.

When Bessie in the morning saw the excellent ladies with their maid about to set to work, she had a great longing to stay at home and help; but reflecting that she had not come all the way to Toledo to mend patchwork, she gave it up. In the evening, the stones of the patio were uncovered, and shining with cleanliness. The great pots containing the oleanders were set back in the middle, but the water-jars remained mysterious in their corner. Overhead, the yellow awning, drawn back for air and light, hung in folds close on one side of the building. It was worked with ropes and pulleys, and could be drawn all or partly across the patio. In fact, the whole establishment was worked with ropes like a sailing-vessel, and the brave señora opened the Bab and hailed the visitors below, like a captain on her quarter deck.

The third and last day was almost wholly devoted to the Cathedral, the real glory of Toledo, not only on account of its religious and historical associations, but from its intrinsic beauty as an example of the pure ingenious Gothic of the thirteenth century.

The Cathedral is said to have occupied its present site before the capture of the city by the Moors. They converted it into a mosque, and in course of time enlarged and adorned it greatly. At the capitulation of Alonzo the Sixth, in 1085, it was agreed that the Moors should still retain it; but this agreement was respected for a few months only, when the Christians took it forcibly from them and had it consecrated as their Cathedral. But of that old building nothing remains. The first stone of the new Cathedral was laid with great ceremony by King Ferdinand the Third, on the fourteenth of August, 1227, and from that time to the end of the seventeenth century, additions and alterations have been constantly in hand. It was the same king who laid the first stone at Burgos in 1221.

The plan of the Cathedral is on an enormous scale, those of Milan and Seville being the only larger churches in Europe. There is no good general view to be had of it, though the towers and dome are very beautiful. The first glimpse of the interior is very impressive; rich in sculpture, but very simple in its lines. The chapels are crowded with sculpture and ornament, and contain often, like those at Burgos, the tombs of important persons. One of these, the chapel of Santiago, has in the centre a grand high tomb, with life-size kneeling figures, one at each angle, and angels holding coats of arms, in panels on the sides. On the tomb repose the effigies of the Constable Don Alvaro de Luna and his wife Doña Juana, who died in the middle of the fifteenth century. Don Alvaro was the prime minister and favorite of John the Second, of Castile. He was something like Cardinal Wolsey, and like him, fell from the favor of his sovereign.

There are also many beautiful inns and brass screens as elsewhere throughout the Spanish churches, and retablos, or large pictures of great height, rising from floor to roof, filled with scenes from the life of the Saviour, richly painted and gilded, with canopies and niches covered with gold. The effect is one of extreme richness and quietness combined. The large windows are mostly filled with stained glass, giving the wonderful charm of contrasted lights and shades, added to that of the colored rays falling through the windows. The walls, which originally were colored, have been sacrificed throughout to the unhappy passion for whitewash, which disfigures everything in Spain.

Now the Horners had to bid farewell to Toledo. Few cities can compete with it in interest, for the grandeur of its position, and the endless picturesqueness of every corner. It gathers up in a small space the whole strange history of Spain so vividly, that any one who could visit its old nooks and corners might work out for himself the whole of it. For here Romans, Goths, Saracens, and Christians, have in turn held sway, and left their mark.

The Horners found time on the way to the station to stop at a shop where the beautiful Toledo work is made; steel, inlaid with gold and copper in lovely arabesque designs. They bought a few "travel presents" in the way of daggers mounted as shawl-pins.

CHAPTER XIII.

VISIGOTHS.

SPAIN is first known in history about the sixth century before Christ, as then inhabited by "Iberi" and Kelts. It is more than probable that both of these races followed previous ones, the existence of which are traced in the flint stone and bronze instru-

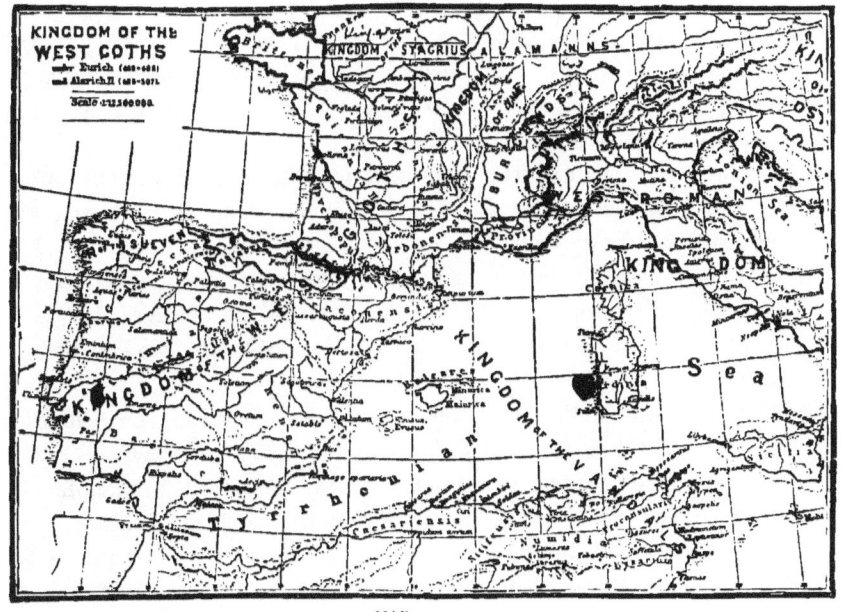

MAP.

ments like those hidden elsewhere in Europe; these were probably also followed by races who built the dolmens and menhirs which are found all along from Algeria to the Orkneys. These Iberi and

Kelts scattered themselves over the peninsula, constantly shifting their ground, perhaps on account of petty wars among themselves, or for now unknown reasons. Both races have left clear traces on the maps of ancient Spain.

From its geographical position, the peninsula was a natural halting-place in ancient times for all the masters of the Mediterranean as they pushed westward. Thus there came successively colonies of Egyptians, Phœnecians and Greeks; and there Carthagenians and Romans met to dispute the supremacy of the civilized world. The Romans occupied Spain for a long period, during which it became nearly as Latinized as Italy; then the Roman Empire fell, and successive waves of barbarian destroyers swept across the land, Sueves, Vandals, Visigoths, wrecking a civilization they could not understand. The last of these races, the Visigoths, strove hard to found an empire from 450 to 710, which, upheld by the real power which in those times kept society together, the Church, lasted, growing, however, weaker and weaker, till it fell before the attack of the Mohammedan Arabs.

These Goths retained the provinces, with their local capitals left from the dominion of the Romans. Their kingdom, in its greatest time, extended far beyond the present limits of Spain, reaching up into France. Seville was at first the royal residence of the Goths, acknowledged not only as the capital of the whole province, but as the metropolis of the kingdom. This honor, however, was in time transferred to Toledo.

The Spanish Goths were by no means the wild, uncivilized people which the expression "Goths and Vandals" conveys. The old Roman organization of the towns was preserved by tradition throughout the whole of the Visigothic times, and the charters, or *fueros*, granted to towns and cities by the kings, founded on recollections of former institutions, are even now in force, and fully exacted.

The government was, in appearance, an absolute monarchy; yet the power of the chief was greatly controlled by the influence of the prelates. The Pope was acknowledged as supreme head of the

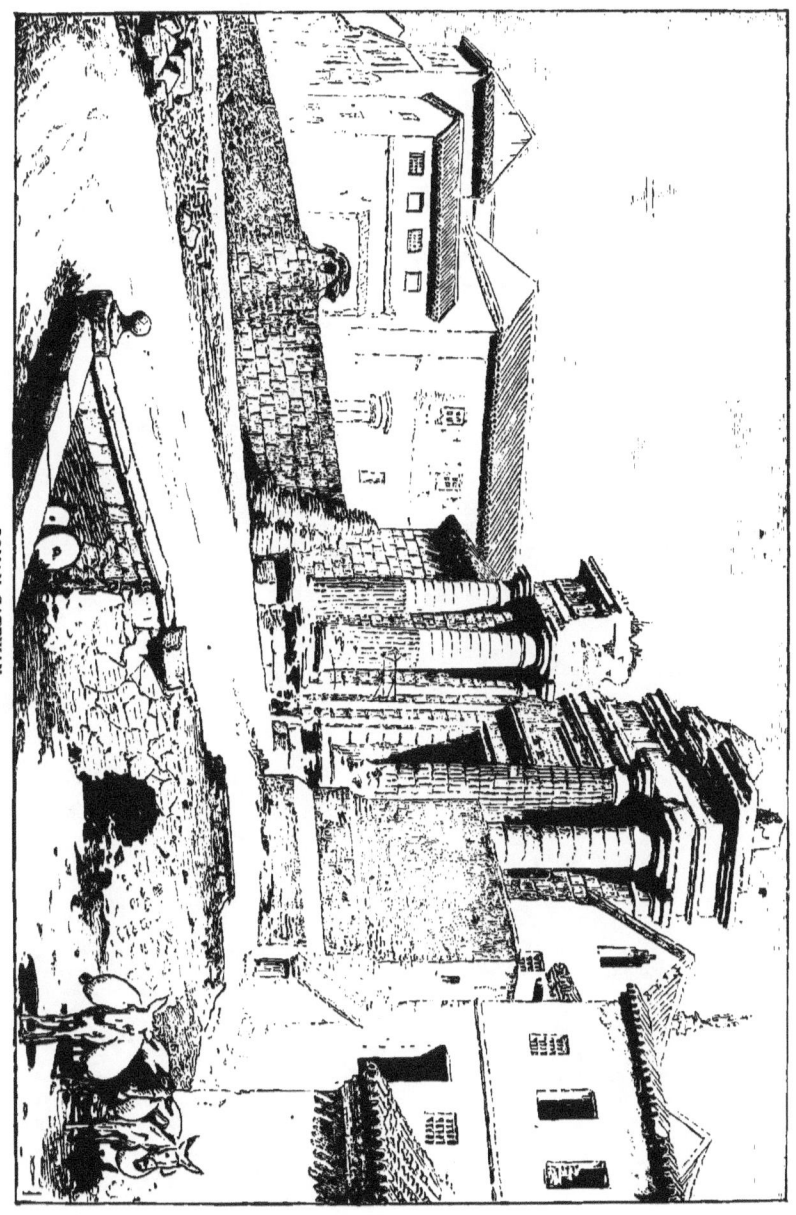
ROMAN GATEWAY.

Church, but the independence of the Spanish bishops was great, and they managed affairs pretty much their own way, in things temporal as well as spiritual, through the national ecclesiastical councils.

The Arian heresy, differing from the true orthodox of the

ALCAZAR IN TOLEDO.

Church, continued about one hundred years in Spain; the disputes arising from differences of faith, made much trouble, as in the following case:

Ermenigild, a certain royal prince, was allowed to share the royal dignity with his father, after his marriage with the princess Ingunda, who was orthodox. But Gosnilda, the second wife of the old king, and therefore stepmother to the prince, was a professor of the Arian sect. The two queens could not agree; the double connection between stepmother and daughter-in-law was too much for them, added to a difference in religion; the one was resolved that her step-daughter should embrace the religion of the Goths, the other that no force on earth should induce her to do so. Gosnilda had violent passions. She so far forgot, it is said, all sense of dignity, as to punish the obstinacy of Ingunda with blows. She seized her one day, says St. Gregory of Tours, by the hair of her head, threw her down, and trampled on her, and afterwards forcibly thrust her into the water to be baptized by an Arian priest. The two husbands finding that their palace was scandalized, agreed to have separate courts; while the elder remained at Toledo, the younger established his at Seville.

Ermenigild soon abjured Arianism, converted by his wife, and embraced the Catholic religion. Warfare followed between father and son, and it ended in an order for the execution of the latter, who had already been thrown into prison; "the ministers of vengeance hastened to the dungeon, and with a hatchet, cleft the head of the prince of the Goths."

This was one of the tales with which Bessie regaled Hubert and Tommy, true to her agreement of throwing light on Spanish history at not too great a cost to her listeners. She had her own method of extracting plums from books of information about the places or people in whom she was interested. She had no strong prejudice in favor of facts, and loved a legend better than a statistical statement. While her dates and statistics were fairly reliable for accuracy, she was quite as likely to introduce a giant or a ghost, as a king and warrior into her narrative, but she had a good memory, and she gave a certain air of genuineness to her account which justified her fondness for romance.

"It is like Mary's water-colors, papa," she pleaded in her own defence, when he once criticised her method of statement; "I must generalize to give a broad effect. Besides, the boys would not listen if I gave them all the arguments for and against the facts."

The story which led her father to demur, was the popular one refuted by serious historians, about the wand of Wamba; Bessie loved to believe it. The Gothic crown was offered to him by the electors, but he was little inclined to accept the dignity. He was an excellent man, who had already filled honorable posts. Prayers and tears were vainly employed to move him. At length, one of the dukes of the palace placed a dagger at his breast, and bade him choose between the sepulchre and a throne. Such a choice was simple, and Wamba reigned.

Such are the facts allowed by historians; but the legend is that when St. Leo, in compliance with the earnest wishes of the Goths, prayed that they might be divinely directed in the choice they were about to make, he was admonished that they must seek a laborer named Wamba, whom they must crown. The soldiers

KING WAMBA.

arriving at his farm found him at the plough, on the confines of Portugal, and gave him the news of his appointment. Thinking it only a joke, he said, "Yes, I shall become king about the time when my staff puts forth leaves again." To the astonishment of all present, the dry wood of the pole he held in his hand was clothed immediately with verdure. Of course they took him away by force to Toledo, and there crowned him.

Wamba made an excellent king. He found the country at war, but soon reduced its enemies. He was obliged to go as far as Nismes, in the south of France, to suppress an ambitious Greek named Paul, who had made himself crowned there.

Hubert pricked up his ears at this, for he had seen the Roman amphitheatre at Nismes, that very summer, and he was pleased to be able to tell them about it. It is an immense building, like the coliseum at Rome, constructed for the same purposes — of combats of animals or men. Many historical phases have swept over the majestic arena, often stained with the blood of human victims. The crescent floated over its walls during the rule of the Spanish Goths, before Charles Martel drove them out in 737.

In the course of time, the place became neglected, and a miserable population which we should call squatters, were allowed to live there. The walls are smoked by the fires they used to cook by. Until the beginning of this century, this superb cirque was surrounded by wretched little houses, and the inside was filled with them; but since then they have been all removed away, and now the amphitheatre, like most of the monuments of France, is not only cleared of rubbish, but restored in such a manner that the original intention of every part can be thoroughly understood.

Hubert was proud to tell his friends about something they had not seen; and Mr Horner was pleased to note the powers of observation of the boy, who had picked up these facts from the guide who accompanied them about the amphitheatre. Hubert could well imagine just the scene when Wamba came and took possession of the place. By royal command, Paul, the conspiring Greek, and the other leading rebels, were dragged by the hair of the head from the vaults of the amphitheatre, and consigned to prison. The merciful monarch satisfied himself with condemning them to wear shaven crowns, and to be shut up within the walls of Toledo.

"Let us enact the scene," said Bessie. "You and I, Fanny, will be leading rebels on account of our long hair, and the boys can be the myrmidons of Wamba, and drag us about."

This brief entertainment took place somewhat appropriately in the room with the green iron door, by which Bessie thought that Roderic the Goth left for good, on the last day of their short stay in Toledo. They had bought their Toledo blades, and taken one last stroll through the irregular streets. After a hearty meal provided by the kind señoras, they were waiting for their guide to carry them to the station for railway omnibuses. He came, and they walked to the square, where they had time for some delicious sherbet in a kind of restaurant, then climbed into a long omnibus which rapidly filled with Spaniards who had been passing the day at Toledo, and were going home by the train; women in mantillas, others with bright handkerchiefs tied about their heads, all merrily chatting together, as a similar crowd might in an American barge.

The Horners arrived at the hotel in Madrid to find Nana and the baby all right, and a letter from Colonel Vaughan.

OMNIBUS TO THE STATION.

CHAPTER XIV.

COMBINATION.

COLONEL VAUGHAN'S letter was addressed to Mr. Horner, with an enclosure for Hubert. He "availed himself gladly," he said, of the proposal contained in Mr. Horner's postscript sent in Hubert's last letter, that his family should continue under the protection of Mr. Horner as far as Gibraltar.

"Well, that is cool!" said Miss Lejeune, when Mr. Horner handed her the letter.

"Rather brief," said Mr. Horner, "but he had a right to put that construction on my offer. In fact, I expected it."

"What did you say?" she asked.

"I merely said that I was going finally to Gibraltar; and that although not yet decided as to my route, or how much time it would take, I should be glad to be a friend to his children, in whom we had begun to take an interest, and that, therefore, I hoped he would let me know how I could be of service."

"That was rather vague," said Miss Lejeune. "What really was your idea?"

"My idea was rather vague," replied Mr. Horner. "I wanted to take them to Toledo; and I thought that would give time for a letter from the father, and he might find it easier to give his directions to me than to a mere boy. Besides"—

"Besides," interrupted Miss Lejeune, "you thought it might come to this."

"Do you much object?" asked Mr. Horner rather meekly.

"Not at all!" replied Miss Augusta. "I think the addition of the children is excellent for both Tommy and Bessie. It was a risk, because we might not have liked them; but there is good stuff in Hubert, and Fanny is a harmless little thing. But " — she stopped and laughed.

"But," said Mr. Horner, continuing her thought, "it is comic that we have burdened ourselves with a nurse and child that we know nothing about!"

"And when," added Miss Lejeune, "we reduced our own party because 'four is enough for travelling in Spain.'"

Mr. Horner assumed a grave expression, although the corners of his mouth had a smiling tendency.

"What will mamma say?" he sighed.

"She will worry," returned Miss Augusta promptly. "I think it will be well not to dwell on the details of the plan until we are fairly out of the scrape."

"We shall come out of it well enough!" said Mr. Horner. "I rely on Nana's intelligence."

"Of course," said Miss Lejeune cheerfully; "all the same, I must say Colonel Vaughan takes his family remarkably easy."

"I rather long to see Colonel Vaughan," remarked Mr. Horner.

ROMAN TOMB.

Great was the joy of the younger portion of the Combination, when the news was announced that they were all to travel together. Nana was full of gratitude. She relieved one serious doubt of Mr. Horner's, namely, the money question. She was provided with an ample letter of credit, and was perfectly sure Colonel Vaughan would not care how much they spent.

"Nor how long we stay away," she grumbled in a tone not altogether meant for herself alone.

Mr. Horner fancied that Nana's heart was full of bitterness toward her master; but he thought it far the best course not to press the subject with her. Time would show, little by little, the true relations of the Vaughans, and meanwhile they were not to be made the subject of idle curiosity.

Children accept all the events of life without surprise. Even Bessie, who was the eldest, thought it a very natural and delightful plan to invite the Vaughans. Tommy and Hubert got on very well together, although each had begun by half despising the kind of boy the other was, or seemed to be.

Miss Augusta regarded the position with some amusement. She soon began to take great comfort in Nana, who, with ready tact, at once devoted herself to her new lady, and to fulfil the little tasks belonging to a maid. Miss Lejeune always travelled without one, but she loved to be waited upon, and she gladly relegated the whole subject of boots, gloves, ruffles, etc., to Nana, who now looked after her wardrobe and Bessie's, as well as that of Fanny Vaughan.

In fact, the plan worked so well that Miss Augusta after a day or two was heard to exclaim to Bessie:

"My dear, I don't know how we ever got on without them!"

But in the beginning it was a little hard for Mr. Horner, whose burden, the luggage, was now nearly doubled. Nana did what she could, but the burden must come chiefly upon one person, who must know how many pieces there are, and exactly where they are. Mr. Horner bore up manfully, conscious that he was the author of the mischief, if mischief there were.

They were now to confront another night journey, and Miss Lejeune's prophetic mind was in gloom at the thought of eight in the carriage, and one of them a baby! "Too ridiculous!"

But when they went up to the place for buying the tickets, Hubert said to Mr. Horner:

"Nana always travels second-class."

"What, and you too?"

"Yes; papa prefers it," said Hubert.

Mr. Horner was puzzled. He had taken first-class tickets to

PUERTA DE LA INCLUSA.

Toledo, by which Hubert had found out that it was the habit of the Horners to travel thus.

It is an excellent plan to go second-class in Germany, and in many parts of Europe, and the Horners as a general thing did so. But in Spain, and especially in night travelling, Mr. Horner was determined to secure all the comforts possible ; in fact, the first-class carriages are none too luxurious. He hesitated now, not liking, at the very start, to separate himself from his charges.

"Why do you doubt?" said Nana. "We go always very safe. Hubert, do you buy the tickets for us, you have money."

This was the sensible plan, of course, and this was the method adopted afterwards. The second-class compartment was very near the one chosen by the Horners for themselves. They saw the others safely disposed in their seats, which were comfortable enough, the only drawback being a row of Spanish hidalgos in mantas, with cigarettes in their mouths; but the Spanish hidalgo is at present a very mild one. And thus Miss Lejeune retained her corner unmolested through the weary night.

It was about two A. M. when they were all awakened by the stopping of the train in a huge dark station, dimly lighted. "Half an hour for refreshments!" is the translation of the cry passed down the platform ; and the Horners all tumbled out hastily, Miss Lejeune in her slippers and sphinx-like veil, Bessie more asleep than awake, Tommy alert, as usual, at the rumor of food. He skipped off to rouse the rest, but the only recruit he could obtain was Fanny; the others were too far gone in sleepiness.

They pressed along with the rest of the passengers to the fonda or buffet, a long dark room thick with cigarette-smoke, and were shoved by the crowd into seats at one of several long tables, set with cups, without saucers, of thick crockery, filled with thick chocolate. Each cup was covered with a flat, round sponge-cake, to be broken and dipped into the brown substance which could not be called liquid. They watched the others, and did what they did, and strange to say, the food seemed to go to the right spot. A full glass of water stood by each cup, to be quaffed after it. No one spoke much; the dark Spaniards with hats slouched over their heads, and mantas on their shoulders, sipped their favorite beverage in silence. Suddenly a wonderful creature, looking like a ruffian, with a bright waist-band stuck full of weapons, passed down the room. He had knives to sell, and daggers, with blades of Moorish curves, and hilts set with jewels, tinsel, in reality, — cheap and gaudy, but delightfully Spanish. The Horners all provided themselves, for a few pesetas apiece, and they brought back from Spain nothing more admired.

Our Americans could not help feeling in a hurry, and they were almost the first to take their seats in the train. They found Nana with the baby, and Hubert, the sole occupants of their carriage; all the Spaniards had taken themselves and their mantas to the fonda.

CERVANTES.

Hubert sat up and stared at them with round eyes.

"Where have you been?"

"Drinking chocolate, thick as mud! And see my dagger!" cried Tommy, brandishing it.

"Oh, I wish I had one! I wish I had chocolate!"

"Come with me, Hubert," said Mr. Horner; "we will go back and you shall have some."

"Oh! is there time?" asked Miss Augusta.

"Time! millions of time," replied Mr. Horner. "I dare say they will not start till to-morrow morning!"

"*Mañana! Mañana!*" (To-morrow! to-morrow!) murmured Miss Lejeune.

They were gone sometime, and Bessie said:

"How mamma would worry! but they are sure to be back."

And so they were, but not until the guards were banging the doors, and urging the *caballeros* to take their places. Mr. Horner popped Hubert into his, and sprang to his seat. The door was

ANCIENT ENTRANCE.

closed, and the train shook. "Did Hubert get a dagger?" asked Tommy.

"No; the man had vanished. Perhaps we shall have another chance."

It was ten o'clock the next morning before they arrived at Cordova, and they reached their hotel in the stupid and owl-like condition to which no practice could make them accustomed. All acknowledged, however, that their nocturnal chocolate had had a good effect, — even Miss Augusta, — who abominated the stuff.

They had passed during the night over the treeless, stony Campos de la Mancha, a name associated with Cervantes, and his hero Don Quixote.

A MONTAINEER ON WAY HOME.
BUYING NUTS.

CHAPTER XV.

CORDOVA.

COAT OF ARMS OF CORDOVA.

"DOWN with the Goth and up with the Moor!" cried Bessie, as they drove to their hotel through the narrow whitewashed streets of Cordova.

"Why do you say that?" asked sleepy Hubert.

"Cannot you see for yourself," asked Bessie, "that everything is changed? This is just as different from Toledo"—

"Different to Toledo, you mean," grumbled Hubert.

There were frequent skirmishes between the children on account of differences in their English.

"Come, children, do not talk before breakfast," said Miss Lejeune. "Luckily we shall have some soon, for here we are."

The hotel was upon a modern square; a minaret of no historic importance, but in the Moorish style, rose before them, and the flat-roofed houses were all painted in gay colors, each story a different tint. A few palm-trees showed their heads here and there.

"How Eastern! is it not?" exclaimed Mr. Horner.

"More Eastern than the East!" replied Miss Lejeune.

The Horners had allowed themselves but one day for Cordova,

as everybody told them the Mosque was the chief thing, and that it all could be done in a short time. This was true, but these single days of sight-seeing are very fatiguing, and should be avoided whenever it is possible.

A good breakfast gave them courage, and after it, they sallied

ENTRANCE TO THE ORANGE PATIO.

forth under the escort of a Moor, the only Arab left in Cordova, by his own account. Nana and the baby, by preference, retiring to bed for a solid sleep of five hours.

They walked in the middle of the street, over rough cobble-stones, sometimes meeting a donkey, but seldom seeing any inhabitants. Occasionally a glimpse through an iron barred gateway showed lovely patios with foliage and fountains; but the streets presented blank whitewashed walls with but few windows. Each frequent turn of the street, excluding any glimpse of distance, shuts in the wayfarer and prevents his gaining any notion of where he is going. It is very easy to lose one's self in the intricacies of a Spanish town, of which Cordova seems the most lonely and deserted. It is as if the inhabitants had vanished, leaving behind them solitude and the shadow of Moorish splendors past.

Having reached the Mosque, they entered first the Court of Oranges, a large enclosed patio with orange-trees planted in it, and at each end a colonnade of marble pillars supporting circular arches. It was so quiet, so Eastern within this enclosure, that they would have gladly lingered there; but their Moor hurried them onward, and in a few minutes they were within the wonderful temple.

The first impression is one of bewilderment and amazement, produced by the maze of pillars, often compared to a roofed-in forest. There are nearly a thousand columns, and wherever one is standing, as in a planted wood of pines, they form receding aisles. They are all of marbles of different colors and kinds,— green and red jasper, and porphyry, black, white, red or emerald. The arches connecting them are in stripes of red and white, which add to the variegated effect of the whole.

It is wonderful, and wholly differs from the Gothic cathedrals the Horners had been seeing. The proportions are low, compared with the lofty aisles of Burgos and Toledo, and the effect new and strange.

They liked less than ever to be led about and made to see details; but their Moor was at their heels. The Mih-rab, or holiest place of the Mosque, they found the most beautiful specimen of Moorish decoration they had seen, not excepting similar places in the East; the rich coloring and gilding are still free from whitewash, which has covered so many Arabian splendors in Spain. Here once was kept the wonderful pulpit of Al-Hakem, of inlaid ivory and precious woods and stones, fastened with gold and silver nails. It was kept in a box covered with gold tissue embroidered with pearls and rubies. This pulpit disappeared not very long ago; but the beautiful Mosaic ornamentation of the Mih-rab still remains

INTERIOR OF THE MOSQUE OF CORDOVA.

to give an idea of its former splendor. In the festivities of Rhamadan, the Mosque used to be lighted with more than ten thousand lamps.

When the Moors entered Cordova after their victory over the Goths, they assured the Christians, as usual, the liberty of their religion, and allowed them the use of their cathedral, built on the site of a temple to Janus. This church was extant in 745.

But soon the population of Moors increased so much that they required more room for their own worship, and they were obliged to take away from the Christians half of their cathedral and make a mosque of it. In 784 Abdurrahman the First bought also the Christian half, determined to build a magnificent mosque, on the plan of that at Damascus, and more splendid than the one at Bagdad.

It must be remembered that this date, of the eighth century of our Christian era, was not two hundred years after Mohammed. The Mohammedan religion, therefore, was in great vigor, and new mosques were being built in the great cities of this faith, with the greatest splendor and display of wealth. This at Cordova was to be the Mecca of the West. The Caliph in person designed the plan, and is said to have worked upon the building himself for a few hours every day. He died, however, the year after it was begun, but his son Hixem carried it on with the same energy, and it was finished in 796, ten years after the first stone was laid. In its palmy days, the roof glistened with gilding and vivid colors, and thousands of gold and silver lamps; its walls were worked like lace, in delicate arabesque, looking like Cashmere shawls, illuminated from behind, and its arches, studded with emeralds and rubies rested on the superbly colored columns. Now the precious stones are stolen, whitewash has obliterated most of the rich coloring, and ignorance and neglect have done the rest.

CHARLES V.

CORDOVA.

On the conquest of the Moors by Ferdinand and Isabella, they had the Mosque purified and dedicated to the Virgin. Several chapels were added, and Charles the Fifth, in his time, allowed the erection of a church within the Mosque, consisting of a transept and choir in the very middle of the interior, amongst the grove of pillars, ruining every vista, and destroying the whole effect of the original plan. It is some comfort to know that when the emperor

WALL OF THE MOSQUE OF CORDOVA.

came to Cordova and saw what had been done, he was very indignant, and said he had no idea that the architects had meant to meddle with the old part.

The Horners were so disgusted with the stupidity of the architects, which allowed them to deface so wonderful a piece of original work by putting anything else inside of it, that they could scarcely look at the elaborately carved pulpits, and stalls, the retablo of jasper and gilt ornaments of the emperor's chapel, all rich and well executed in the sixteenth century. Other Spanish churches in other places they might admire, but not this misplaced specimen. After they left the cathedral, the Moor took them to the site of the Caliph's palace, of which nothing now remains but a few walls and orchards. There is a modern house with a garden containing some trace of the old water-works; they wandered through shady alleys, overhung with neglected rose-bushes and pomegranates in blossom. The nespola was ripe, an odd fruit, like a little pear with a stone in the middle. They sat upon a bench above a large stone tank in which carp were swimming, and tempted the fish to rise by throwing in to them little bits of stick and flowers, as they had no bread, or anything to make crumbs with. Great lazy creatures came and poked up their noses at the bright geranium petals, and whisked

BRIDGE OVER THE GUADALQUIVIR.

away contemptuously, but they did not tell the rest, for others kept coming. The Moor gathered little bunches of flowers for the ladies. It was very pleasant to sit in the shade, and see the bright sunlight and sky. Before them rose the walls of the Alcazar Nuevo, now used as a prison.

This Alcazar was once the palace of the Gothic kings, where the Caliphs lived afterwards, repairing it and enlarging it. Moorish writers describe its wonderful gardens and halls, and its baths provided with water brought from the Guadalquivir through a brick hydraulic machine. These baths lasted until the end of the fifteenth century, when the huge wheel which supplied them with water was destroyed, because its noise kept Queen Isabella awake, when she was established in the Alcazar.

From an arbor in the terrace of the garden all overhung with grapevines then in blossom, could be seen the bridge over the Guadalquivir, of sixteen arches, very picturesque, with a many-sided tower beyond it. Miss Lejeune made a little pencil sketch of it in her note book, while the boys and Fanny took a second excursion around the weedy paths of the rambling, neglected garden. Bessie leaned against the parapet looking off on the hot midday landscape, and dreamed of the Caliphs of Cordova. The Moorish guide, awaiting them, sat upon the lowest of the steps leading to the arbor, and hummed little Arabic songs that reminded them of the East. This midsummer dream was disturbed by Tommy, who came running up, saying:

"Fanny don't feel well. I believe she is too hot. She is sitting on the steps over there!"

Miss Lejeune shut up her sketch book at once.

"She has been running about in the heat too much," she said. "Where is your father?"

"Papa! papa!" called Bessie and Tommy with one breath.

"He is somewhere in the gardens," said Bessie, "he will find us."

They hastened, the guide following, to the place indicated by Tommy, and found poor Fanny, now looking very white, sitting on a stone step, and leaning against the trunk of a palm-tree which happened to be there. Hubert was wetting her forehead with his handkerchief which he had dipped in the carp pond.

"I feel so dizzy," moaned Fanny.

Mr. Horner now approached from another direction. "Poor child! it is the heat," he said; "we must carry you home."

He stooped to lift her in his arms, but the guide put him aside, and bearing the little girl well and firmly, led the way back to the hotel.

CHAPTER XVI.

ANDALUSIA.

MOORISH KNOCKER.

BESSIE'S letter to Mary will describe the rest of their day in Cordova.

"Now you must know that at breakfast a stout man sat opposite me with whom we had nothing to do until I took a piece of cheese and began to eat it before engaging upon an orange. The man now accosted me, and said in French, that it was dangerous to do that, as the two things did not join well in the stomach. This began a friendly conversation, which was followed up by an invitation to see his strawberry garden.

"So after we came back from the Mosque and Alcazar gardens, although we were most dead, we took a carriage and drove to his place, on an open sort of boulevard near the railway, modern built, and quite different from the winding whitewash of the Moorish streets. He was a most dear man, the Gefe of mechanicians of the railroad. You must pronounce Gefe as if you were going to say hay-fever, but stop short of the last syllable. He is Alsatian, but his wife, from Malaga, speaks only Spanish Her mother, however, came originally from Germany, and we tried a little of that language with the old lady. If you could have seen us all hobnobbing in these languages, and receiving handsful of the most delicious fat roses, jasmines, orange blossoms, gilly flowers, larkspurs, pansies, all the time our radiant host telling us how he loved to have us see his garden, which owes its luxuriance to intelligent irrigation. A little fountain was playing in the middle of it, and little rivers trickled everywhere with bright borders of grass dipping in them. His strawberry bed bears all the year round; and a muchacha was set to gather strawberries the minute we got there; and by and by when it was high time to come away, we were led into the house where there was a piano they forced me to play on — me! I played —

Way down upon the Swanee River,

and they thought it was beautiful. Anyhow it filled up the time till a repast of fruit was prepared. The Gefe took great oranges from his own tree, cut them in two, squeezed them like a sponge, and the juice poured out over the strawberries heaped up in a big dish, with lots of sugar. This is the true way to eat them, in a land where both fruits are really sweet. But fancy the strawberry of commerce, at home, with a sour Valencia orange squeezed over it! Not all the sugar at Park & Tilford's could sweeten that combination. He brought out his own wine from his own grapes. It was not first-class, but the intention was good, as you say about a bad water-color; we all touched glasses and sipped, and finally came away with expressions of mutual and undying regard. You can't imagine what a dear man he was, and he behaved exactly as if we were the only people he had ever loved."

Bessie and her father were the only Horners who enjoyed this episode of Cordovan hospitality, for Miss Lejeune was not sorry for the excuse of staying at home to look after little Fanny, and the boys declined the formality of a visit. When they heard afterwards of the feast of strawberries, they all thought perhaps they had made a mistake.

As for Fanny, a cool dark room, and sound sleep on a comfortable bed, soon restored her. Probably the heat had overcome her.

Nana, refreshed by a quiet morning, was cheerful and active, and sat by Fanny's bedside during the rest of the day, while the boys looked after the baby, and amused her with playthings in the salon of the hotel.

They were glad to go to bed early, after the uneasy night before, and the long sight-seeing day; moreover, they were to be called at four the next morning, to take the train at six o'clock for Seville.

Cordova was the gem of the South as long ago as Roman times. Under the Goths it lost its importance, but regained it under the Moors, who made it the capital of their part of Spain. The wealth, luxury and splendor it contained at that time was like the descriptions in the Arabian Nights; it lasted through various changes of Arabic rule until the thirteenth century, when it was captured by Saint Ferdinand, and lost all its prosperity, which it since has never recovered.

CHURCH OF SAN PABLO, CORDOVA.

In spite of its Moorish attributes, Cordova is now a good Christian city, and under the especial protection of the Archangel Raphael, in whose honor a huge monument was erected a century ago. On top of a column the archangel stands, a sword in hand, with outstretched wings, and bright with gilding, like a sentinel watching over his city. Below the column is an artificial mound of rock-work, about which a horse, a lion, and a sea-monster are grouped in a grotesque and tasteless way, with four allegorical statues. It is said that the archangel appeared in person before a certain priest of Cordova in his chamber, and said to him: "I swear to you that I am the Angel Raphael, and that God has given to me the guardianship of this city." This happened in 1578, and in commemoration of it the monument was made later. The words of the angel,

RAPHAEL'S PILLAR.

in Spanish, are inserted upon its base. In Cordova the Horners first understood the real patio, which is at its best in Andalusia; other square courtyards they had seen which bore the name, but they were not to compare with the brightness of the one into which their Moor led them from the dull street.

A patio is not merely a court, it is not only a garden, but a court, garden, and a parlor all in one. Between this one and the street was a narrow passage, or vestibule, paved with marble, flanked with columns, surmounted with bas-reliefs, closed with a *grille*, or gate, of light iron railings gracefully designed. Opposite the entrance was a statue; in the middle a fountain was playing and a palm-tree and orange-trees were growing; chairs and tables, vases of flowers, books and work were scattered about, just left by the people of the house, who there could enjoy the charms of ourdoors life with all the seclusion of an interior. Above was an awning which might be drawn over the top if the sun should intrude too far.

Miss Lejeune was delighted with this lovely specimen of a patio.

"We must have them at home," she exclaimed; "why not? We might build them in New York just as well as here."

"Instead of back yards!" said Tommy.

"I'll tell you how we could manage it. The Grillsons and we could run our back yards together."

This was Bessie's plan.

"It would be best," said Mr. Horner, lending himself to the project, "for four houses to combine, do not you think so? Two on each street, whose yards touch as ours does with the Grillsons. Then instead of that narrow back street which the grocer's carts frequent, there would be a series of patios, with houses running about the four sides.

"Yes," continued Bessie, "and there could be Moorish arches underneath the houses for the carts to drive through."

"It would not be nice," objected Miss Lejeune, "to have all the carts and the rag and bottle men coming through our patio when we were taking our *siestas*."

PATIO OF A PRIVATE HOUSE, CORDOVA.

ANDALUSIA.

"And I should not want the Grillson boy to have the same patio with us," said Tommy.

"Oh, well!" said his father, "if there is that difficulty, we shall have to wait until we love our neighbors as ourselves before we introduce patios in New York."

The ride from Cordova to Seville was lovely in the early morning, for they were fresh from a good sound sleep in their beds, and could enjoy it. The road was bordered with hedges of agave and cactus, the tall flower stalks of the former shooting up as high as the telegraph poles, for which they might serve if they were only permanent. The ones just preparing to blossom looked like huge asparagus stalks, Fanny said; others more advanced spread out side shoots like the branches of gigantic candelabra. All the land was covered with verdure; by the running streams masses of pink oleander bloomed and marked their course; the fluffy blossom of yellow acacia perfumed the air, and its sweet scent floated in at the open window.

In short it was Andalusia! Andalusia, the land of romance and sunshine, the most beautiful province of beautiful Spain.

Andalusia embraces the whole of Southern Spain, and its farthest cape is the extreme southerly point not only of Spain, but of Europe. One chain of its mountains, the Sierra Nevada, contains the highest summits of the peninsula, and its river, the Guadalquivir, from Seville to the ocean, is the only stream of real service for navigation in the country. The wines and olives of Andalusia, its grapes, and oranges, and fruits of all kinds, are the finest, its horses and cattle are the best, its bulls are the fiercest of all Spain. Its cities are famous for their attractions, and its men and women for their grace and beauty. All things take on an air of loveliness in this land of warmth and glow. The Moors left a deeper mark here than elsewhere, for they kept their beloved realm of Granada long after they had lost the rest of Spain.

The people of Andalusia partake of the lightness and joy of their climate; with them all is joy, light, wit, *dolce far niente.* Life is pleasure; they puff their *cigarito,* strike their guitar, and pass their days with song and laughter. Their manners are superb; even the beggars in the street raise their hats with courteous elegance. If the natural defects accompany this character; if they lie, and steal, and are lazy and cowardly, it is a pity; the Horners were inclined to see the charming side of them, and disbelieve the other. They are superstitious, but devoted to their religion; the churches are frequented by devout and earnest worshippers.

CHAPTER XVII.

EARLY SPAIN.

ANDALUSIANS.

VERY early, the Mohammedans reached in Spain a higher degree of civilization than in any other part of the world. At its outset, its successes were brilliant; the military spirit and discipline which it established among all classes gave to the nations who embraced it the appearance of a vast, well-ordered camp, and the importance it gave to combat and conquest was peculiarly well adapted to the character of the wild tribes among whom they were preached. The successors of Mohammed, called Caliphs, represented both his spiritual and temporal authority. It was their duty to lead the army in battle, and on the pilgrimage to Mecca. Their authority had all the force of divine sanction, and their ordinances, however weak or wicked they might be, became laws which it was sacrilege to disobey.

Within a century after the coming of Mohammed, their apostle, they had already set up their religion over vast regions in Asia and on the northern shores of Africa, and arrived before the Straits of Gibraltar, ready for the invasion of Spain, led thither by their love of conquest, their long career of victory, and the rich spoils offered by the Gothic monarchy.

After the fatal battle of the Guadalete, fought in the summer of 711, which ended in the slaughter of King Roderick and the flower of his nobility, the Goths never rallied under one head, though they made enough resistance in various strong positions to postpone for three years the final conquest. Their conquerors were liberal. Such Christians as chose, were permitted to remain in the kingdom and worship in their own way, and to be governed mostly by their own laws; in short, they were much better treated than the Moors were afterwards by the Christians, when their turn came to have the upper hand.

ARMS OF SEVILLE.

Having thus made for themselves a foothold on the Peninsula, the Moors pressed farther forward into Europe, with the ambition probably of carrying the banner of the prophet to the very shores of the Baltic. True believers flocked to the white standard of the house of Omeya from the farthest parts of the dominions of the Caliphs; and the whole Mohammedan world contemplated the expedition with the deepest interest. But their progress was checked by the far-famed defeat at Tours, in 733, where a combined army of Franks, Germans, and Belgians marched upon them, led by the great Charles Martel, who here won his title of "The Hammer," in memory of the blows he gave his enemies on that occasion. The contest of that day was long and bloody; when darkness arrived it was undecided, and all night the Christians remained in their tents under arms. At dawn they prepared to renew the struggle; the white tents of the Arabs extending far on every side, were still there, but not a living creature came out to meet them. The enemy had abandoned their camp, and silently slipped away. Christendom was saved. The churches were filled with people of all ranks, thanking Heaven for so signal a victory.

Thus cut off from conquest in Euorpe, the Arabs began to quarrel among themselves, and their overgrown empire was broken up. The province of Spain was the first to secede; and the Omeya family occupied its throne as independent princes for three centuries, ruling wisely and well. The race of the Omeyades need not shrink from a comparison with any other dynasty of equal length in modern Europe. Their long reigns, peaceful deaths, and the unbroken line of their succession, prove the justice and wisdom of their sway. Their princes of the blood were intrusted to the care of learned men, to be instructed in the duties of reigning; they were encouraged to compete in the academies of Cordova for the prizes of poetry and eloquence, and frequently carried them off.

The splendor of this dynasty was shown in their palaces, mosques, and hospitals, and their admirable system of irrigation which still fertilizes the south of Spain.

Their fountains and aqueducts rivalled those of Rome.

MANOLA.

These works were scattered all over the country, and devoted to the adornment of Cordova, their favorite residence and capital. The wealth of the Mohammedan princes of that age was immense, and their superiority in useful arts and industry perfectly well accounts

ANDALUSIAN SERENADE.

for it. The sovereign had for his share one fifth of the spoil taken in battle, and one tenth of all the produce of the country.

He often engaged in commerce on his own account; and mines belonging to the crown brought to it a large income.

But the best mine of the Caliphs was in the industry and sobriety of their subjects. The Moors introduced into Southern Spain various tropical plants and vegetables whose cultivation has departed with them. The silk manufacture was largely carried on by them, and with fine fabrics of cotton and woollen, made an active commerce with the Levant and Constantinople, spread by means of caravans all over Europe. Alhakem the Second is a good specimen of a despotic sovereign employing his power to promote the happiness and intelligence of his race. In his tastes, love of knowledge, and munificent patronage, he was a kind of Medici among the Moors; he encouraged literature in every way, and amassed for himself a library said to contain six hundred thousand volumes. Writers swarmed over the Peninsula at this period; not only men, but women, devoted themselves to letters. Scholars from all parts of Europe, Christian as well as Arabic, came to Cordova; for this period, brilliant for the Mohammedans, corresponds with that of the deepest barbarism of Europe, when a library of three or four hundred volumes was a great thing for the richest monastery.

But this greatest prosperity was followed by sudden decay. Alhakem died in 821. During the life of his successor, the Empire of the Omeyades was broken up into a hundred little states, and the magnificent capital, Cordova, dwindled into a second-rate city. Now was the chance for those Spanish monarchs to assert themselves, who, during all the Moorish period, had retained in the North their titles and successions in a direct line from Roderick the Goth. By the ninth century they had reached the Douro and the Ebro, and by the close of the eleventh, under the victorious banner of the Cid, they had advanced to the Tagus.

With Hixem the Third (A. D. 1031) ended the Caliphate of the West and the noble race of the Omeyades. From this period to the establishment of the kingdom of Granada, there was no supreme chief of Moorish Spain. The part of the country, ever growing less, which was free from the approach of the Christian armies, was governed by petty kings; and by the middle of the thirteenth century, its constantly contracting circle had shrunk into the narrow limits of the province of Granada, where, however, on a comparatively small point of their ancient domain, the Moors erected a new kingdom of sufficient strength to resist for more than two centuries, the united forces of the Spanish monarchies.

Meantime, while the Moorish dynasty in Spain was rising to so great a height to fall so low, Christian Spain, for several hundred years, had been nothing but a collection of little states, always quarrelling with each other. At the close of the fifteenth century, these various provinces were blended into one great nation, under one common rule, strong enough to overthrow its enemies, and eject from the land the race alien to its religion. By this time, the number of states into which the whole country was divided, was reduced to four :— three Christian, Castile, Aragon and Navarre,

FOUNTAIN IN THE ALHAMBRA.

all belonging to a common faith, though not united in government, and Grenada, the sole remaining Moorish kingdom.

Aragon at that time included Catalonia and Valencia; to the crown of Castile had fallen all the other provinces except little Navarre, which, shut within the Pyrénées, continued to maintain its

BALCONY IN SEVILLE.

independence when the rest of the smaller states in the Peninsula had been absorbed in the dominion of either Castile or Aragon.

Castile, from an early time, held the first place over all the other states, and when at length they were consolidated, the capital of Castile became the capital of the new empire, and her language the language of the court, as of literature.

From the beginning of this period, the nation which had been corrupted by the long prosperity of the Gothic reigns, experienced the salutary influence of adversity. Entire reformation of luxurious habits was necessary when a scanty subsistence only could be earned by a life of temperance and toil. Thus grew up the real Spaniard, from the stock of the Goth, but with new qualities of endurance and heroism, a sober, hardy, independent race, prepared to demand its ancient inheritance, and to lay the foundation of a better government than that before known.

Their struggles with the Moors, and their own discussions, delayed the growth of this people; but at length their long wars with the Mohammedans kindled in their hearts the glow of a united patriotism; their ardor for religion became intense, fed by their aversion to that of the foe.

Thus patriotism, religious loyalty, and a proud sense of independence, founded upon knowing that they owed their possessions to their personal prowess, became characteristic traits of the true Spaniards. The spirit of chivalry kept up by traditional ballads and legends, possessed in those times Spaniard and Moor alike. The Spanish knight became a hero of romance, wandering over his own land, and even into farther climes, in quest of adventures. This romantic spirit lingered in Castile long after the age of chivalry had become extinct in other parts of Europe, until its illusions of fancy were dispelled by the satire of Cervantes, who makes of his hero, Don Quixote, a burlesque hidalgo in search of adventures, yet describes him with so charming a style that we love him while we laugh at him, and do not cease to reverence the spirit which influenced the age of romance and chivalry.

CHAPTER XVIII.

SEVILLA.

DELIGHTFUL weather followed the Horners to Seville, and justified their choice of May and June for travelling in Spain. Delightful rooms, also, they had in the Fonda de Europa, in the Calle Sierpes, which means Serpent street, and well it deserves its name, from its winding course. They had to descend from the railway omnibus at the entrance to the street, for it is too narrow for driving, and posts are put up to prevent vehicles from entering. So they followed the guide through the narrow street full of foot passengers and flower-stalls, to the entrance of the hotel, and their baggage was brought after them on wheelbarrows. The hotel was a rambling sort of place, a part of which had once been a convent; there were convent stairs leading down by a broad sweep to the patio, where a fountain was playing, with gold fish in it, and banana trees and oranges were growing.

The patio was surrounded by a sort of arcade, under which little tables and sofas were placed, where the guests might have coffee in the morning, or sip their after-dinner demi-tasse. The dining-room opened on this patio, a long, low place where thirty or forty people breakfasted and dined. The Horners enjoyed this table d'hote, for there every variety of nationality was represented, and the talk was always animated in several different languages.

A very vivacious Italian, who was evidently an old stager, delighted in discussions upon the politics and religion of Spain, and he was equally ready in French, Spanish or German. English he protested he could not manage, and his efforts to get on in that language with an English lady who sometimes sat next him, were very amusing. The food provided was very good, and now the Horners were becoming used to a good deal of oil in the cooking, and to seeing the fish turn up in the middle of dinner.

It seemed somewhat odd now to have Hubert and Fanny domesticated in the bosom of the Horner family; at first there were some little hitches in the way of discipline, for the English children, both of them, were a little inclined to take their own way about what they ate and where they went; but the Horner rule was so light that they soon yielded to the gentle sway of Miss Lejeune, and the controlling glance of Mr. Horner.

"Not a third orange, I think, Fanny," Miss Augusta had to say

DESERTED SQUARE.

once, and Fanny put down the one she was taking from the dish with a start, surprised that her doing so had been observed. The other children considered Fanny to be rather greedy, and probably she did eat too much, for she looked thin and pale, and suffered from indigestion sometimes, a thing unknown to the healthy Horners.

Their rooms overlooked the patio, and across the tops of banana-trees and the blue striped awnings below, to a kind of terrace with a carved railing on which stood plaster busts at intervals, rather the worse for wear, and flower pots set between them full of bright geraniums and other gay flowers. Upon this terrace the señoras came and went, who did the washing on top of the house. Spanish politeness calls every maid and washerwoman a señora. There were two delightful old hags who performed this function at the Fonda de Europa, and the children became very intimate with them; for this roof, reached by a long flight of shaky steps from the terrace, was their favorite resort. It was a series of flat roofs rather than one, and a little house was built up on it for washing purposes. While Miss Lejeune was sketching there, taking advantage of the shade furnished by this little hut, the señoras stood at their tubs scrubbing the clothes, and chattering and laughing in the liveliest Castilian. The younger of them appeared to be about one hundred and fifty years old; but was probably less, for women of that class begin to look old early in Spain, as in the East.

The señoras were very friendly with the boys, and encouraged their acquaintance with a dark little Spaniard, the son of the proprietor. He had a kite like many other Seville boys, who were to be seen tending these broad square playthings on other roofs. The kites soared about above the spires and domes of Seville, and stood out dark against the glowing sky where the picturesque Giralda rose not far off.

Much as they liked their hotel, the top of it was their favorite part; and, after a day of sight-seeing, they often climbed to the roof and sat leaning against strong parapets which offered themselves most conveniently for their backs, resting and rejoicing in the lovely Andalusian atmosphere.

They settled themselves for a week or more in Seville, tired with the hurry of Cordova, and the crowded impressions of the brief stay at Toledo. The weather was still so fresh and cool that they felt safe on that score, and Seville was one of the places which they had promised themselves to thoroughly explore.

So every one was permitted to take out from trunks and boxes the little luxuries of life; and before the first day was over, their large and pleasant salon was littered with everything which could make it seem homelike. A large round table in the middle of the room was heaped with guide-books, novels, dictionaries and writing materials; the blotting-cases of each member of the party found a place there, with sketching blocks and paint boxes. A huge

CATHEDRAL GATE.

mañola, ten inches across or more, which Bessie had bought, a bud, at the flower-stall in Serpent street, spread itself over the tumbler it stood in, and filled the room with its fragrance. The great bouquets given them by their kind Gefe at Cordova, adorned the room, still fresh, for a day, after which they were given to the señoras to throw away; but these aged crones, choosing each a bright, though somewhat faded, carnation, stuck these flowers in their hair with true Andalusian coquetry. How they laughed and wagged their old heads when Bessie praised them.

GIRALDA.

"Oh! would it not be nice," exclaimed Bessie, as they came back to their room after almuerzo, "if we had not to go out and see sights. I like this room just as well as all the rest of Seville. I believe I will stay here all the time, and look across the patio and merely go up on the roof occasionally."

She was stretching her feet out comfortably before her, having thrown herself into a remarkably easy chair, with her hands clasped over her head.

"Very well, my dear," said her father. "Do as you like. We will tell you all about it when we come back. But as Juan is waiting for us below, those who intend to do the Alcazar to-day must be ready soon."

"Does Nana know we are going out, Fanny?" asked Miss Lejeune of the little girl who was leaning over the railing of the wide window, looking down at the paroquets and other birds in the court below.

"She's down there with baby," said Fanny, calling "Nana! Nana! come up and dress me to go out!"

"Well, I may as well exert myself," said Bessie, who was the last to be left behind on any occasion. "Where are my boots?"

As often in Spanish hotels, two dark bedrooms, side by side, opened by glass doors upon the salon. It is not a bad arrangement, as it shuts out bedroom characteristics during the day, and at night the doors can be thrown open for ventilation; but the want of light in these places makes the whereabouts of boots, hats, and gloves, somewhat doubtful, except to the most methodical. Thus it was some time before the party could be got together.

"Now where are the boys?" asked Mr. Horner, returning from his room which was on the other side of the corridor, looking on a mysterious den where turkeys were kept, and hens and chickens, and where great rats shared the food of these fowls.

"Were they not with you, papa?" asked Bessie.

"No; I have not seen them since breakfast."

"I will go up on the roof and look for them," suggested Fanny.

"No; because then you will be lost!" said Mr. Horner, with a little impatience. "Did not they know we were going out?"

"Oh, yes, papa! I dare say they are down at the door with Juan already."

And so it proved; only that when they arrived at the door, although the two boys were there, Juan, tired of waiting — it was now an hour after the time appointed for him — had "just stepped round a corner for a moment."

Calle Sierpes is all corners; so it was difficult to follow the guide. A servant of the hotel being summoned, hunted him up after a further delay of about five minutes, and then the party was under way, crossing the sunny plaza, almost deserted at this hot time of day.

GIRALDILLA.

"It is so hot and so sunny," said Miss Lejeune, "do not you think we had better postpone the gardens of the Alcazar?" she asked, after a little pause.

Juan pronounced that early morning would be a better time for that.

"Then let us simply take a turn through the Cathedral," said

Mr. Horner; "we can, too, if we like, climb to the top of the Giralda."

"Do not count me for going up things!" cried Miss Lejeune, shaking her head.

"Aunt Dut, they say this is very easy," said Bessie; "it is made for horses; you can do it perfectly well."

"Are you sure it was not made for donkeys, my dear?" demanded Miss Augusta.

They had now reached the square of the Cathedral, and the pretty tower of the Giralda, which serves as its campanile, was before them.

It is called La Giralda, from the revolving weathercock on top; a bronze figure representing Faith, called la Giraldilla. It is a vestige of the mosque which once stood where the Cathedral is now, and was built as a muezzin tower. The warm rose-color of the brick of which it is built, combined with white stone, and inlaid tiles of green, gives a light Oriental effect which is very charming.

"Tommy," said his father, "it is said that this was built by the man who invented algebra, which was named after him, for his name was Geber."

"I wish he had never invented it," growled Tommy.

CHAPTER XIX.

ANOTHER CATHEDRAL.

WHEN the chapter began the present cathedral in 1402, they decided to erect a church so large and beautiful, "that coming ages will say we were mad to attempt it." The last stone was laid in 1508, a century having been devoted to the task.

There are different styles in different parts, but the main body inside is strictly Gothic. All the styles and all the arts have combined to produce here their first effects. The Moorish Giralda, the Græco-Roman exterior, give variety and prepare the eye for the beautiful Gothic arches within, where the paintings are by some of the greatest masters, the stained glass among the finest specimens known, the sculpture beautiful, and the jewelers and silversmiths' work is rare and unrivalled.

The first impression on entering is one of awe and reverence. There is a sublimity in the sombre masses and clusters of spires, whose proportions and details are somewhat lost in great shadows which pervade the place, among the lofty naves and countless gilt altars. Vast proportions, unity of design, severity and simplicity of ornament, give the Cathedral at Seville a place among works of real genius in architecture.

This huge square building is on a platform with a broad paved terrace running all around, ascended by steps. The pillars belong to Roman temples and the old mosque. There are nine entrances of different styles and periods. One of the most remarkable is the Puerta del Lagarto, so called from the crocodile placed there. This was sent to Saint Ferdinand by the Sultan of Egypt, amongst other curious animals, many of which died on the way, and were stuffed and placed in the cloisters. The Puerta del Pardon leads to the Court of Oranges. Its high horseshoe arch and its bronze doors are Moorish, built as early as 340 A. D.

The Court of Oranges is a huge paved patio, with a fountain

INTERIOR OF CATHEDRAL.

in the middle; here are seen the projecting sides of the transept, and the airy, flying buttresses springing from one nave to another, with open-work, richly decorated pinnacles, little pillars and domes full of variety, movement, and beauty.

Within, there are nine naves, aisles supported by graceful pillars surmounted by Gothic arches. Like the Cordova mosque, it seems a forest, but a different one. This might be a grove of stately maples, while that suggests a wood of sturdy pine-trees. The choir, as usual in Spanish churches, blocks up the central portion; but there is so much space around it that it seems but a detail, for there are so many long vistas unencumbered by any obstacle from one end of the church to the other.

The first dome of the Cathedral fell in the night, December, 1511. Great was the consternation at the news; and every town sent its own architect to repair the misfortune; to him of Salamanca was given the glory of replacing it, and thus completing the Cathedral as it now stands.

The chapels are full of sculptures and paintings

PUERTA DEL PARDON.

enough to tire the eye and brain before the round has half been made. Over the altar in one of the Chapels there is a mysterious solemn picture of the Descent from the Cross, ascribed to a pupil of Michael Angelo. It is said that Murillo liked this picture so much that he desired to be buried before it. He used to stand for hours looking at it; and he once replied to some one who asked what he was doing:

"I am waiting till those holy men have taken down our Lord."

His own works adorn the chapels of the Cathedral, and nowhere in the world do they give so fine an effect, as here among the solemn influences and grave shadows of the consecrated pile.

The Conception, by Murillo, in the Chapter House, Miss Lejeune considered the most beautiful and wonderful of his works; it is placed nobly, hung high above the ground, and surrounded by a profusion of delicate carvings. The Virgin's expression is exquisite, the coloring perfect.

One of the chapels contains a picture with a peculiar and exceptional interest. It is one of Murillo's grandest paintings, called St. Anthony of Padua. It is very large, and fills an immense space on the wall, and is separated from the spectator by the railing of the chapel, which is itself dark, while a strong side light falls upon the picture. The Saint is kneeling and stretching his arms toward the vision of the

HOLY MOTHER.

infant Jesus, who descends toward him amid cherubs, and flowers, and sunbeams. Below this bright group of immortals, is seen through a vista the cloister of the convent, dark and solemn by contrast with the radiance above. The figure of the Saint occupies about one quarter of the canvas, which, seen from the first, appears harmonious and perfect; but a close examination from the side shows that it has been joined and patched, and that the place occupied by the principal figure must have been at one time empty. This is the painting, which, by a bold theft, was deprived of its most important part.

One morning when the custodian of that portion of the Cathedral came to it, Saint Anthony was gone; actually cut out of the can-

SEVILLE HOUSETOPS.

vas, whose ragged edges revealed a barren space. The excitement was intense, not only in the Cathedral, but all over Spain; in fact, all over the world which recognizes the value of Murillo's work, and the daring of such an attempt to convert it into money. Before very long the canvas bearing the Saint was presented at the New York Custom House. It was strictly detained there, and afterwards returned to its proper owners. Saint Anthony has been restored to his place in the picture; the edges are so carefully joined that it cannot be considered injured; and so his unexpected journey to America and back, lends a new interest to the principal figure.

The Horners could not begin to see all the wonders of painting, carving, and gilding, at one visit to the Cathedral. Fanny was soon tired, and pleaded to be left to rest on a bench near one of the chapels. The others soon joined her, and Bessie said joyfully:

"Come, Fanny, are you rested now? We are all going to the top of the Giralda."

Mr. Horner and Miss Lejeune followed, coming away thoughtfully from the study of Zurbaran's pictures in a dark chapel. The boys were hunted up, and they all came forth into the bright sunlight.

"I think the way will be," said Miss Lejeune, "to do the interior in bits. As we are to be here so long, it will be lovely to drop in quietly and look at the pictures and different chapels."

They all agreed that this was the best plan, and when Bessie set herself, in the evening, to read the description in the guide-books, she found mentioned tombs of kings, and sceptres of monarchs, and figures of saints which they had seen nothing of.

As it happened, however, the time in Seville flew by so fast, and was so divided between sight-seeing and sweet repose upon their roof or in their convent-patio, that there were but one or two hurried visits to the Cathedral.

Miss Lejeune found the ascent of the tower easy enough, even for her. The steps are very low and flat, so that it is like moving up an inclined plane, turning at each of the four corners of the square tower. From the windows of the gradual ascent, the buttresses and light crenelations of the cathedral wall were seen in detail. At the top a wonderful view burst upon them. The crowded, narrow streets, and tiled roofs of Seville were at their feet. They could trace their way to the square near Serpent street, and recognize the location of their hotel by a great Churrigueresque church near it, which formed the attractive foreground of their view from the hotel roof.

ANOTHER CATHEDRAL.

TORRE DEL ORO.

The later architecture of Spain, beginning with that of the sixteenth century, is generally denounced as in the decline of art, an overloaded, highly-colored style, combined with fantastic shapes and ornaments. To give color, even on the o u t s i d e of roofs, domes and spires, glazed tiles, called *azulejos*, of blue, red and yellow are freely u s e d, whose g la ncing surfaces reflect the light like glass. Churriguera, an architect of the seventeenth century, used this style and made it general, and his name, which is given to it, is considered the synonym of bad taste. But in spite of the bizarre forms and bright tints of it, Bessie and Miss Lejeune both dared to admire it with them, it was equivalent to praise when they exclaimed:

"Churrigueresque!" misapplying the name, very likely, to anything they liked of a florid style.

They looked from the Giralda across the Guadalquivir to the broad stretching country beyond, and below them, on its bank, they saw the Torre del Oro, or Tower of Gold, so called from the orange azulejos which once gave it the appearance of a brazen or gilt tower.

GARDENS OF THE ALCAZAR.

It has, moreover, been used by Moors and Christians as a treasure house, and they were told that in the time of Columbus, the gold he brought from the New World was deposited here.

They looked across the square and down upon the formal gardens of the Alcazar, which they were impatient to visit, and the long gallery running along one side, now decayed and impassable, but once the place of many gay and brilliant scenes.

"Oh! let us go to the Alcazar to-morrow!" cried Bessie, and all the children longed to be running about in the stiff alleys set with box and cypress-trees, with here and there a tall palm, which they saw below them.

"But the picture gallery!" exclaimed Miss Lejeune; "we must not leave Murillo any longer."

"You saw Murillo enough, aunt Dut," said Tommy, "to-day in the Cathedral."

"Only enough to make me thirst for more," said Miss Lejeune.

"There is plenty of time," said Mr. Horner; "we might"— "divide," he was about to say, when all the great bells of the Giralda, close above their heads, began to ring at once with a tremendous clangor. They fled in haste, and the only question was, which should first reach the bottom.

CHAPTER XX.

JUSTA AND RUFINA.

DURING Roman rule, Seville was a magnificent and prosperous city, as the vestiges of many splendid monuments still show. Julius Cæsar entered the city in August, 45 B.C. Seville was the centre of a sort of pagan worship, and the only city in the Western world where there were temples to Venus, whose effigy used to be borne through the city, in procession on the shoulders of the noblest ladies. As this imposing statue was one day being carried along the streets, two Christian sisters, Justa and Rufina, who were selling earthenware jugs, refused to do reverence to the idol as it passed; upon which the bearers dropped it right in the middle of their pots and pans, and instantly determined upon the death of the girls. Thus they became martyrs, and the patron saints of Seville, and are so represented. Murillo has painted a charming picture of them, surrounded by their earthenware, and holding the Giralda between them.

Afterwards the Goths made Seville their court and capital, until they gave this distinction to Toledo, as we have seen. After the battle of the Guadalete, and the rout of the Goths, Seville kept out the Moors during a month's siege, but yielded at last; and Abdul-Azis, who ruled over it for some time, married the widow of Roderick.

The family who held the splendid Caliphate of Cordova, controlled Seville until they fell a prey to the feuds which divided the powerful and alternately successful tribes of Almohades and Almoravides. Meanwhile Seville was prosperous, and, next to Cordova, the most important city in Spain.

The treason of rival Moorish races, and the petty jealousies of their rulers, were paving the way gradually for the Christians. King Ferdinand, the Saint, in 1247, at the head of the flower and nobility of Castile and Leon, laid siege to the city, and the Christians entered it, after fifteen months' resistance, in 1248.

In the Royal Chapel of the Cathedral, the lower part of the altar is formed by a silver glazed receptacle containing the almost perfect body of Saint Ferdinand. It is displayed twice a year, with the ceremony of military mass, etc. The king is dressed in his royal robes, with the crown upon his head; his hands are crossed upon his breast. Upon his right and left are the sword and sceptre which he bore.

It is said that upon the usurpation of the Christians, a population of four hundred thousand Moors, Jews and Arabs abandoned the city. Some of these settled in the neighboring towns, but the greater number hastened to the new kingdom of Granada.

By this time, the Spaniards, once but a little band driven by the Goths to the mountains, had grown to be a powerful and united nation. The separate provinces had either given over their mutual quarrels, or yielded to the superior force of the strongest among them. Leon and Castile were united under one head. Ferdinand the Third was lord of Spain from the Bay of Biscay to the Guadalquivir, and from Portugal to Valencia. At that time the Christian kings were at peace for the moment. Ferdinand had suppressed conspiracies, and subdued all rivals to the throne, of whom the chief was his own father. The crusade against the Mohammedans was published by the archbishop, and the same indulgences granted to those who assumed the cross in Spain, as to those who visited the Holy Land. Toledo and Cordova first fell into the hands of the Christians, and then came the turn of Seville.

This conquest was the last achievement of Ferdinand. He died in Seville four years after its surrender. He was a just and able ruler, and a valiant soldier, but cruel and bigoted, like the rest of the kings of his time, setting fire with his own hands to the fagots for burning heretics. Nevertheless, it was probably for such acts,

FOUNTAIN IN THE ALCAZAR.

rather than for his prayers, fastings, and frequent disciplines, that he was canonized several centuries after by the Pope.

Seville now became the court of the Christian kings. It was Alphonso, the son of Ferdinand, who gave to the city its badge which is still seen on many buildings, carved into the stone-work. The figure in the centre represents a hank or skein, called in Spanish *madeja*, so that the whole reads:

NO M'HA DEJA-DO.

which means, "she has not deserted me." King Don Pedro the Cruel, who held court in Seville about a century after Saint Ferdinand, had left there many traditions of his bloody tyranny. From his accession to the throne at sixteen, one murder quickly followed another; he killed every one who interfered with his pleasures, and shut up his queen in a fortress, where she was poisoned, or killed, by his orders. This unfortunate queen was Blanche of Bourbon, of the house which has since furnished many kings to France. Her great-aunt had married half a century before, the sixth son of King Louis the Ninth of France. Fair Blanche

MOORISH ARCHES, ALCAZAR.

was summoned from distant Bourbonnais to be the bride of the king, Don Pedro, Seville; but he only married her for political reasons. He scarcely looked at her, and after forty-eight hours, he went away, and perhaps she never saw him again. He kept her shut up in a convent and in prison, and when she died, it was under great suspicion of poison or dagger.

Such conduct brought him into difficulty. His cruel treatment of his queen, and of his half-brothers, caused revolt and insurrections, but he lived with his favorite Maria de Padilla in great splendor and luxury in the Alcazar until the time of his destruction came.

LA SALA DES EMBAJADORES, ALCAZAR.

At last Don Enrique of Trastamara, his half-brother, returned suddenly to Spain with a strong band of French adherents, and drove Pedro out of his kingdom. The general voice was in favor of Henry, and he took possession of the throne. After such cruelty to Queen Blanche, Don Pedro could not hope for aid from France, but Edward the Black Prince, who was then in Gascony, took up his cause.

"Wasn't that strange!" exclaimed Bessie, when she was telling these things to the boys, whom she had succeeded in securing as listeners. They were all sitting in a row on the roof of the Fonda de Europa, with their backs against a chimney, watching swallows and kites soaring about the rosy shaft of the Giralda, which stood out warm and dark against a glowing sunlight.

"Our splendid bold Black Prince joining with that hateful murderous Don Pedro the Cruel!"

"I know about the Black Prince," said Hubert, "he was English."

"Of course," said Bessie loftily, "but he had great possessions in France, and if you English had kept up his prowess you would not have lost them all!"

Hubert looked as if he was sorry, but could not very well help it; but Tommy put in:

"Well, tell more about Don Pedro; I rather like him."

With the splendid army of the Black Prince to help him, Pedro totally defeated Enrique; but when the Black Prince had gone off, Enrique returned and finally triumphed. Pedro was captured, and confronted with his brother; a struggle ensued between them.

> Henry and King Pedro clasping,
> Hold in straining arms each other;
> Tugging hard and closely grasping,
> Brother proves his strength with brother.

All the knights held back and watched the struggle, till one of Enrique's followers, seeing his master overthrown, seized Pedro by the leg, which gave his opponent the upper hand, and he stabbed the king to the heart.

This is described by Froissart, and also in the ballad just quoted, which was translated by Sir Walter Scott for Lockhart's Spanish ballads.

No one was left to lament King Pedro but his once proud favorite, Maria de Padilla.

> The utter coldness of neglect that haughty spirit stings,
> As if a thousand fiends were there, with all their flapping wings.
> She wraps the veil about her head, as if t'were all a dream,
> The love, the murder and the wrath, and that rebellious scream.

> For still there's shouting on the plain, and spurring far and nigh,
> "God save the King — amen! amen! — King Henry!" is the cry,
> While Pedro all alone is left upon his bloody bier,
> Not one remains to cry to God, "Our Lord lies murdered here!"

The next day, in consequence of Bessie's tales from Froissart, and quotations from the Spanish ballads, the boys were in a great hurry to visit the Alcazar. They made an early start after coffee, to avail themselves of the freshness of the morning.

It is a portion of a Moorish palace, and its style is purely Moorish, with beautiful horseshoe arches, and surfaces adorned with arabesque work. The grand façades glitter with gold and vivid colors, and the pillars are of precious marbles. Much of this lovely work had been almost concealed by whitewash, but this has recently been taken off, and the Alcazar repaired, at the expense of the Duke of Montpensier.

In the splendid Hall of Ambassadors, there is a series of portraits of the kings of Spain from Chindasvinthus to Philip the Third. The next room is the one where Pedro caused another half-brother, Don Fadrique, who had been invited by him to come to a tournament, to be murdered. Stains of blood on the marble pavement are still shown to the traveller, but the Horners had learned not to shudder at such marks, not likely to be anything but iron-rust. But they did shudder at the story, and at the strange poem, one of Lockhart's Spanish ballads, which makes the unfortunate Fadrique in the beginning tell his own story, until the order for his execution is pronounced, when the sequel is given in another voice.

The party after seeing all the rooms of the palace, scattered themselves about the stiff, but charming, alleys of the large garden, which gave them infinite pleasure. Pomegranates, roses and jasmine were all in blossom, hedges of box and ivy of great size testified to their long growth, as well as the large palms and yew-trees. Stiff rows of myrtles and orange-trees stood in green boxes along the walks, and made pretty vistas, adorned with trickling fountains. Miss Lejeune was delighted, and promised herself and the girls to spend many a morning there.

CHAPTER XXI.

ITALICA.

FOR the afternoon, Juan, the guide, proposed a drive, and as no one was tired but Fanny, the plan was approved, and Fanny was quite willing to be left behind with Nana. The cool and pleasant patio always recommended itself to the nurse as a suitable spot for looking after her charge, and there the grave, industrious French woman, sat willingly for hours, sewing interminably, knitting or darning stockings, while the contented baby, still so-called, played by her side. The children often brought home amusing toys and trifles for the child, who, indeed, had been so accustomed to Nana's society from her birth, that she required no other. Fanny now proposed, however, to help Nana amuse the baby, and Nana announced that she had a letter to write, a serious undertaking with her limited knowledge of writing and spelling.

The rest started off in the best of spirits, in an open carriage rather crowded, to be sure, for Juan was on the box with the driver; but it was large, and held very well Bessie, wedged between the two boys on the back seat, while Miss Lejeune and Mr. Horner occupied the places of honor.

It is difficult to drive through the narrow streets of Seville, for they are wide enough only for one set of wheels between wall and wall, with no allowance of sidewalk for foot-passengers; an arrow at every corner shows in which direction carriages may pass through each street, a direction always so faithfully obeyed that no one knows what would happen if it were not followed; so that if two carriages should meet face to face "one of them would have to drive over the top of the other," said Bessie.

"They would both have to turn round," said Hubert.

"But they could not turn round, either of them," objected Tommy. "What would they do, Juan?" he continued, applying to the guide on the box.

"It never happened," replied Juan, and with this they had to be satisfied.

They went first to see a private house belonging to a great duke, called the Casa de Pilatos, or House of Pilate, because it is said to have been built in imitation of Pilate's house in Jerusalem, by the Marquis of Tarifa, who made a pilgrimage to the Holy Land in 1578, and erected this palace on his return. The Horners thought there was no resemblance in the rich Moorish building to the House of Pilate, so-called, now standing, which they had seen in Jerusalem; but this did not prevent them from admiring the one before them.

Beyond the Guadalquivir, a pleasant drive along its banks, and by a palm grove belonging to the ancient Abbey of Santo Ponce, they came to the only vestige now left of Italica, a ruined amphitheatre, in the ancient city, founded by Scipio Africanus, as a home and resting place for his soldiers wearied after the campaign against the Carthaginians. Three Roman Emperors were born there, Trajan, Adrian, and Theodosius. Its palaces, aqueducts and circus were magnificent. The palace of Trajan was partly preserved until 1755, when an earthquake destroyed their last traces. Coins are still often dug up, and a beautiful pavement is known to have been taken up and preserved by a poor monk less than one hundred years ago, but no one knows now what has become of it.

Very little is left of the amphitheatre but the graded walls which mark its vast dimensions; but Hubert was more excited over it than anything else he had seen, as he was familiar with the arena at Nîsmes, and he liked to point out to the others how it differs, and how it must have looked before the massive sides were shaken by earthquakes and before sand and weeds had encroached upon its enclosure. As the Horners had never been in Rome, they had never seen the Coliseum there, which is built on the same principle; but

ROMAN AMPHITHEATRE AT ITALICA.

every one is familiar with its form and plan by seeing photographs and reading descriptions. The rooms where the gladiators used to prepare themselves for combat, and the dens which contained the wild beasts, have been discovered only lately.

The drive through the bright sunny air was delightful as the party returned to Seville. They were in the best of spirits, for they had that day received a budget of letters, which had been sent first to Madrid, so that there had been a delay of a day or two before they reached Seville.

Mrs. Horner and Mary wrote glowing accounts of their retreat in the Pyrénées. Philip, who, it had been feared, might find it dull, was going up all the mountain peaks in the neighborhood, either on foot, or on the good little donkeys which were always ready to be hired. Mary was sketching daily, and every day growing visibly stronger, and Mrs. Horner's energies were absorbed by an immense affghan she had begun to knit of Barege wool, a staple of the country, which is very soft and pretty. They had received long letters from Mr. Hervey before he sailed from America on the first of May.

"I must write Mary a long letter wholly about the pictures," said Miss Augusta; "I have only just hinted at those we have seen in the different cathedrals; but as soon as we have been to the gallery here, I shall give her a full account of it. I do wish she could see it with us!"

"So do I," said Mr. Horner; "but I think her rosy cheeks and good appetite are much better for her than a feast of Spanish painting."

"What sort of a boy is Philip?" asked Hubert. "Is he like you, Tommy?"

"He is bigger than I am," said Tommy, "and in some respects superior. I don't know whether you would like him better or not."

Hubert too had a brief letter from his father, and one enclosed in it from his mother, quite old as to date by the time he received it, as it had been sent to Gibraltar in full faith that the children would have reached there. It was a short, but sweet, affectionate letter, written with the feeble hand of an invalid. Nana shook her head as she looked at it.

PALACE OF THE DUKE DE MONTPENSIER.

"*Pauvre madame,*" said she; "*elle est très malade.*"

The driver brought his party back to the hotel through the gay Corso de las Delicias, wide and modern, like the Prado at Madrid, and they passed the entrance of the palace of the duke de Montpensier, which, with its gallery of pictures and beautiful gardens they did not have time to see that day They came back to it, however, for a long examination before they left Seville.

The Duke de Montpensier is the uncle of the present king; that is, he married the sister of Isabella, the deposed queen. Also the sweet daughter of the duke, Mercedes, the first wife of this king, Alphonso, was the pretty young queen of whom the people were so proud, that they grieved sincerely at her early death.

The palace, called San

GARDEN AT SAN TELMO.

Telmo, is very handsome, and is surrounded by spacious gardens full of orange-trees, palms and shrubs, pines, and many rare plants, very charming to wander in. Long alleys of tall sycamores were crossed by others of pointed cypress, underneath which, and everywhere, were lovely flowers, roses, jasmine, and all early summer things. White peacocks trailed their dainty feathers upon the hard sand of the walks; they looked like fine ladies with white satin trains. There was no color, such as we commonly call "peacock color," anywhere upon them; but the eyes of the feathers were indicated by a different tint of white. There was a real stork sitting on his nest on top of a pillar, set up on purpose for him, apparently.

The children were delighted with this immense garden; they passed a whole morning there, Nana sitting in a Moorish summer house, on an island in a lake, while Miss Lejeune sat by her side sketching. Nightingales filled the air with their sweet notes, which all the Horners were too light hearted to consider melancholy. The nightingale seems a cheerful bird when he is jug-juging away in the general feathered chorus on a sunny noon, in broad sunshine. His note really sounds not in the least like "jug-jug," being sweet and melodious as possible; yet somehow these words, always used to describe it, seem to do so. With the usual open hospitality of personages in Europe, the duke allows strangers to visit the inside of the palace. The rooms are handsome, and in them are to be seen the pictures of the Montpensier collection which came to America some years ago.

Miss Lejeune looked at these with great interest, remembering that they had not pleased the general taste of those who saw them in Boston where they were shown, and that she herself had found them severe and unattractive in subject. Now that she had seen a good many Spanish pictures, and moreover, many fine masterpieces elsewhere in Europe, she was glad to modify her opinion. She thoroughly enjoyed the Piedad by Morales, and four subjects in the life of Christ, by Zurbaran. The pictures are well hung in rooms whose light and decorative surroundings are in perfect harmony with them. However, Mr. Horner and Miss Lejeune had a good laugh at the inconsistency of human nature, which allows itself to be so differently impressed at different times, and under different influences.

"Consistency is a poor virtue," Miss Lejeune remarked. "I love to find that I can enjoy those pictures now so much more than before."

"Consistency should not, certainly, be allowed to interfere with progress," remarked Mr. Horner.

The weather was growing decidedly warm; every day as the Horners came home from excursions, they found it agreeable to stop at a cooling drinks shop, which stood in the plaza near the end of their narrow Serpent street. Chairs were always offered them, where they sat, while a small child, who could hardly reach to the counter, prepared the *horchata*, or squeezed the *limon*, the mild beverage beloved of the Spanish.

CHAPTER XXII.

MURILLO.

ALL of one morning was spent in the picture gallery by the older portion of the party, while the boys and Fanny went back to the Alcazar gardens under the protection of Juan.

The gallery is small, consisting only of one long room or hall in a building, formerly a church and convent. It is especially devoted to Murillos; and here first may Murillo be studied to advantage. Side by side his beautiful and world-renowned Madonnas hang, in number, and near them, pictures on other subjects by him, which have never been copied or produced elsewhere. Photographs of them are to be bought in Seville and Madrid, but they are as yet very little known, except to Spanish travellers, and students of Spanish art. Murillo is the pride and the true head of the Seville school of painting; he shares with Velasquez the highest honors of Spanish art. He was born in Seville, probably in 1618, on the first of January, nearly twenty years after Velasquez. As he inclined early towards painting, he was put in the hands of Juan del Castillo, a painter still celebrated for some fine portraits, and for being the teacher of masters greater than himself.

When Murillo was twenty-four years old, a fellow artist returned from London bringing with him a style of painting learned from Van Dyck. Murillo, on seeing this, much desired to go to England; but Van Dyck died about that time; he would have liked to study in Italy, but money was wanting, even for the shorter journey to Madrid. The latter place he attained to, by painting and selling a number of devotional pictures. Arrived at the capital, he presented himself to Velasquez who received him with great friendship. He was thus able to study and copy the great works of Titian, Rubens, and the rest belonging to the royal galleries.

When he returned later to Seville, all wondered at his skill, and

MURILLO.

from that time forward his reputation increased until his death. In 1674 he finished eight great pictures for the church called La Caridad, which contains a fine collection of his works.

The coloring of his pictures is extremely soft and lovely, harmonizing with the same expression in the faces of his Madonnas, and the beautiful little cherubs he delights to paint.

He died in April, 1662, after falling from a ladder where he was painting the Marriage of St. Catherine, in a church in Cadiz. He was not killed, but fatally hurt, and was carried back to Seville to die.

Bessie found she liked the Murillos much; had she not, she would have been difficult to please, there is so much variety in the grouping of the personages he represents, and such pretty types of children, fine ones of old men, etc. The Virgin of the Napkin is so called because it is said to have been painted by Murillo on a dinner napkin, as a gift to the cook at the convent at Cadiz, when Murillo was at work there. In spite of her fondness for legends and her faith in the marvellous, Bessie did not believe that they had napkins as big as that picture at the Capuchinos, a couple of centuries ago.

Seville honors the memory of her great master, and there is a monument to him before the Museum which contains the picture gallery.

Miss Lejeune found time to describe the Murillo pictures to Mary in a long letter which she said the rest could skip if they felt inclined. It also dwelt on the delights and difficulties of water-color sketching in an atmosphere so brilliant and so different from our own. Miss Lejeune was an enthusiast for art and sketching, although she despised the results of her own efforts. She never expected any praise for her sketches, and rather preferred not to have them seen, although she was good-natured about showing them.

Mary, on the other hand, was likely to become a proficient in the pretty art. She wrote of lessons that she was taking of an excellent teacher who happened to be staying at their hotel in Luz; he painted in a wet, broad style that she especially liked, and was not unwilling to pick up a chance scholar, so apt as Mary proved herself.

One day Juan took the children through an old quarter of the town, where a fair was going on; everything under the sun set forth for sale on little tables in the middle of the streets—

pottery, brass work, cheap handkerchiefs, stockings, a collection gay in color, and arranged not only to show the best effect, but also to tempt the purchaser.

Tommy bought a handful of ripe mulberries for Fanny, which looked to the others a little repulsive, as they were jammed, though juicy; the only thing at hand to put them in was a chance piece of torn newspaper Passing through the market, they saw lovely ripe figs. The man that owned them was sound asleep stretched at full length behind his counter, and Juan had to poke him with his umbrella to rouse him to a bargain.

Juan was a Spaniard, but dressed to resemble an Englishman, in a closely buttoned pepper and salt coat, with trousers to match. He always carried an umbrella, and invariably smoked a cigarette. His voice was low, and his English was distinct and grammatical, with some limitations, for his knowledge went no farther than the range of his duties as *valet de place;* but he was honest and intelligent, and always kind to the children, who became very fond of him, and amused him much by their views of things Andalusian.

They went one night to a theatre, open, though it was summer; not the most splendid of Seville, but a bare, barn-like place, like a town hall in a country town. Every one was smoking cigarettes. A *perro* came and smelt of Bessie, and then sat down on a seat in front of her for the performance. There was first a little play of modern life, and then a pretty ballet, with good dancing and suitable dresses, the orchestra playing light and charming dance music, of which the movement and melody become very dear to travellers.

The Horners had a tiresome time finding, or rather losing, their way back to the hotel, for Juan was not with them. They thought they knew it, and went round and round, expecting each corner would lead them to Serpent street, until their feet were very tired with walking upon the round stones. At last they reached a square which they knew to be their square, with the opening to their little street just opposite to the direction where they had expected it to be. The next day, tracing as well as they could their course on the map, it seemed as if they had carefully avoided Calle de Sierpes at every turn.

This was somewhat mortifying, for they had been there ten days when it happened, and felt quite at home there. They were all growing very fond of Seville, and it was hard to think of going away. They were now beginning to pick up a little Spanish, and Bessie, especially, could make herself understood in shops and in the street.

Mr. Horner was the first to put into words the general feeling that the party must be moving on.

"I told them at the banker's in Madrid, to forward our letters

NUNS AT PRAYERS.

to Seville only a week," said he one morning. "So we must not expect any more here. There may be a budget at Granada now, I think."

"So soon!" exclaimed Bessie. "Why, papa, it is only a minute since we came."

"Just a week," said her father; "and ten days since we left Madrid."

"Oh, dear!" she replied; "and every place we have been to here we want to see over again."

She was just then writing a long letter to Philip, and Miss Lejeune and Mr. Horner were engaged in the same way, all sitting at their large round table, at little oases which each had made by piling up or pushing away the things that were heaped upon it.

"I have been talking with Juan about our course," resumed Mr. Horner; "he says the steamers are excellent from Cadiz to Malaga; indeed, that we could keep on, and go by sea all the way up the coast of Spain; but of course we do not care to do that. I wish we might see Palos, and something more of the traces of Columbus."

They had, of course, not failed to think of the discoverer of America in Seville, and where there are many things to recall him. In the pavement of the Cathedral is a marble slab bearing an inscription to the memory of the second son of Columbus, a man of learning, who bequeathed his library, called la Colombina, to the chapter, and his ashes to the Cathedral. On the slab is written:

A CASTILLA Y A LEON.
MUNDO NUEVO DIO COLON.

"To Leon and Castille Columbus gave a New World."

It was the great glory of the reign of Ferdinand and Isabella, that under their auspices America was discovered; the queen especially undertook the enterprise when it had been declined by others, and served Columbus in the most acceptable manner by supplying him with ample resources.

"Shall we say day after to-morrow, Augusta?" continued Mr. Horner.

"So soon!" she said with a sigh looking round the room which, with all its paraphernalia of pleasant living, looked too attractive to leave. "Yes, I suppose so; do you know what time we start?"

"At noon, Juan says. That is a good thing; and there is no night travel this time."

"Not till we are upon your favorite steamer," said Miss Lejeune, putting down her pen, and rising.

Mr. Horner shuddered. He did not share the fondness of some of his family for aquatic excursions.

"But, aunt Dut, you needn't put on your hat now!" remonstrated Bessie.

"No, but I want to see Nana about the washing. I think the señoras took some this morning, and they must be told to bring it back in good time."

So the Seville season came to an end. Their happy establishment was broken up, and they set off for Cadiz one bright morning after almuerzo.

AT AN OLD WELL — WATERING THE LAND

CHAPTER XXIII.

CADIZ.

MISS LEJEUNE and Bessie were just alike in one respect, which made them, on the whole, excellent travellers. They always were very unwilling to leave the place they were in, and went about packing and breaking up with gloomy energy; but once in the train, their spirits rose, all regret was cast aside, and they found it delightful to be moving again. No fatigue disheartened either of them, and they both regarded the arrival at a new hotel as one of the chief delights of travel.

In this they differed from Mrs. Horner and Mary, who rather dreaded the worry of being established in new rooms. The mamma especially always feared beforehand there was going to be a smell, or that the bed would be hard, or that the view would not be satisfactory. She concealed these fears, but was not quite happy until a new day in a new place proved that they had been unwarranted. The two sanguine ones, Bessie and Miss Augusta, had it their own way in Spain; for papa's two anxieties, one about the baggage, which always came out all right, and the other the boys, who always turned up in time, were of no account.

Juan escorted them to the station, and there they parted from him with much regret, for he had been very useful, and had become a valued friend; but they felt now quite capable of relying upon their own resources.

They were seated in the train by two o'clock P. M., but it did not start until four, after the usual Spanish fashion, and thus it was late before they arrived at Cadiz, and they approached the city in the dim faded lights of after sunset, over a long, very long causeway, with water on each side. Cadiz has been compared to a guitar, connected with the rest of the world by the handle. The Horners rejoiced at seeing the sea after many weeks, and the salt fresh air of the Atlantic was delightful to them.

Cadiz is a walled town; the railway station outside. They drove through an arched gateway, guarded as usual, by the inevitable pair of alguazils, and, before moving on, had to undergo a parley with custom-house officials; nothing was examined, however, and they were free to pass on to their hotel, through straight, long streets, which appeared wide and modern, after sinuous Seville.

"Just like Philadelphia!" declared Bessie, who was old enough to be taken to the Centennial there, in 1876.

Cadiz, however, is not much like Philadelphia. Their hotel was on a pretty square, planted with trees, and in the light of the street

ALGUAZILS.

lamps people were flitting about, strolling in groups, or chatting on benches, for the night was soft and warm.

Miss Lejeune leaned from her balcony and enjoyed the novelty of the scene, and the tinkling sounds which rose from guitars. After the shut-in, close walks of Seville, the sense of space was very agreeable. She looked up at the bright dark sky, full of stars.

The rest of the party were too tired for sentimentalizing. Fanny was put to bed at once; the others waited for dinner to be ready, which deserved rather the name of supper, for it was after nine before it was served, and then they went directly to bed, defying digestion, for there was to be an early start in the morning, the steamer which they were to take, being advertised for six o'clock.

So not much after dawn the sleepy set were roused, and soon found themselves on the stone pier, bargaining, through the medium of an interpreter from the hotel, for a row boat to take them out into the bay.

"I am so glad mamma is not here!" said Bessie, as they settled themselves into a large boat with ample accommodations.

"This boat is solid enough to please her," said Mr. Horner.

"It looks," said Miss Lejeune, "as if it were made of the original beams left over from the ark."

Two strong sailors, with sashes round their waists, and *panuelas* tied about their heads, pulled the heavy boat over the water with swift strokes.

"Imagine Columbus," exclaimed Miss Augusta, "being brought in from his caravel!"

"His caravel was not so much larger than this craft, I suppose," said Mr. Horner.

The steamer was lying far off from the town, and in the half-hour's pull to reach it, they had a pretty view of the receding city, very white in the morning light, rising from the water with graceful domes and spires.

This was all they saw of Cadiz, once the most famous seaport of the world, under the Romans; less important in the hands of the Goths, and afterwards of the Moors, its prosperity rose again with the discovery of America, for it shared with Seville the deposits of gold and merchandize from the new country. This made it a frequent point of attack from pirates and princes coveting its treasures; and it has repeatedly been plundered and almost destroyed. Its wealth and commerce were great, even to the end of the last century. French invasion and civil war have reduced its importance, and it is now less interesting a place for tourists than many other places, because its monuments and works of art are fewer. It contains, however, in the Church of the Capuchins, the fatal pict-

A LADY OF CADIZ.

ture which caused the death of Murillo. It is just as he left it; not quite finished. Cadiz, like Seville, is famous for the beauty of its women.

The *Cristoforo Colon* was a large clean steamer, comfortably arranged. As there were but few passengers, the Horners had the pleasant deck pretty much to themselves, and the boys were soon running all over the ship, exploring its mysteries. Miss Lejeune fell into conversation with an elderly gentleman who spoke French so fluently, and had such old-fashioned elegance of manner, that she guessed him to be a Frenchman. He had travelled much in Spain, and knew all about the pictures, and talked very well about art.

By and by when the boys had come back, the old amateur rose and soon left her side, and Hubert took his place. Tommy carried Bessie off to see the live stock. Fanny was in the cabin with Nana and the baby, and Mr. Horner was smoking and reading somewhere by himself.

OLD AMATEUR.

Hubert was in a state of excitement natural enough as he approached the end of his journey. He was restless, but at the same time he wanted to be quiet, and did not really care for the sights of the ship, which amused Tommy.

Miss Augusta took his hand and held it a little while, leading him to talk about home and his mother, and she now learned more of these matters than at any previous time.

"You cannot think how lovely mamma is," said he in a low tone; "and her voice is so gentle and dear." His eyes filled with tears as he went on telling how sweet and patient she was, and how delicate.

"I have her photograph!" he exclaimed, "and I never showed it to you. Tommy has seen it. I look at it every evening just before I go to sleep."

He brought the little picture up to her. Miss Augusta saw a very pale wan face, with large eyes looking forth from it, a sweet expression, and graceful shoulders and pretty hair drawn back from the forehead. She sighed as she looked; she could not help it.

"I know, I know!" cried Hubert; "you think mamma is very ill. But we thought going home would cure her. To England, I mean, — to grandmamma's. That was taken in London to send to papa. But mamma wanted to come back, and so we started, but she could not come any farther than Bordeaux, and then they said — they said" —

He broke down; he could go no further. Miss Lejeune understood the rest.

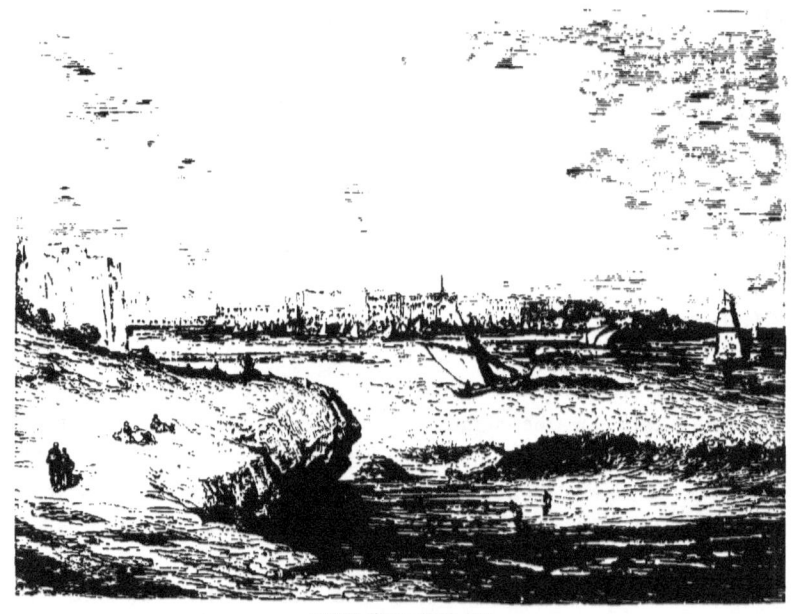

CADIZ FROM THE SEA.

"Do not try to tell me, dear boy. I know. Has she always been an invalid?"

"Ever since baby was born. Did you know baby was born in India?" he asked, his face brightening with the change of idea and the thought that Miss Lejeune would be interested.

"Papa was in India before he was stationed at Gibraltar," he went on, "and mamma went there with him; but we did not go. Fanny and I stayed at grandmamma's. It was ever so long ago that they went. I scarcely remember about it. And then I remember when they came home. It was so funny to know papa and mamma; and papa was very different then. It is only lately that he has grown so gloomy" —

He stopped short. Probably he was thinking, as Miss Augusta was, that it was anxiety about his wife that had changed him.

"Poor Colonel Vaughan!" she murmured to herself.

"Poor papa!" said Hubert, "he has lots of trouble. Mamma's sister died only a year or two ago, and she was just the same as papa's own sister."

The tears were coming again. Miss Lejeune was beginning to feel that she must not let him dwell longer on these sad themes, when the other children came breathlessly up, crying, "Come and see Africa; it is just ahead!" The whole party assembled at the very most forward part of the ship, and there, to be sure, were the blue mountains of Tarifa, and the shore of another continent. They stood there watching the land on each side of them, for some time. In one place the width is but twelve miles.

> It is a narrow strait,
> I see the blue hills over,

sang Bessie.

"Well, Tommy," exclaimed Miss Lejeune; "only think of our being together a second time sailing through the Straits of Gibraltar!"

CHAPTER XXIV.

THE NARROW STRAIT.

IN fact, Tommy felt important on account of his previous passage of the strait, and did the honors not only to his own party, but to the group generally, pointing out the fort and lighthouse of Tarifa close at hand, and distant Tangier across the water.

Gradually moving westward, they entered into stiller waters, and before them loomed up, really majestic and grand, and bristling with cannon, the great rock on which proudly waves the flag of England.

Hubert now began to feel at home, and could point out to Tommy many objects which had not come to that young gentleman's knowledge on his short visit of the year before.

Letters and a telegram had been sent to inform Colonel Vaughan of the approach of his family, and they were full of excitement at the thought of meeting him. Fanny clung to Nana's hand. Hubert stood by Mr. Horner, trying to think of some proper way to express his sense of the kindness he had received.

"All right, my boy," said Mr. Horner; "you have behaved very well, and it has been a great pleasure to us all to have you with us."

He was himself a little anxious, and indeed a little curious to see the father of these children with whom he had so unexpectedly come into such close relations.

There are no children who need to be told that Gibraltar is an English possession, and that the English have held it fast in spite of every effort to regain it by Spain, who naturally begrudges it to a foreign power. It has always been a bone of contention, and between the Moors and Spaniards, had sustained eleven sieges before the time when, in the course of the war for the Spanish Succession, it was seized by Sir George Rooke, July 24, 1704, who took possession of it in the name of Queen Anne.

In June, 1780, a desperate and skilful attempt was made by the united land and sea forces of France and Spain to destroy the little English squadron which lay in the harbor. Six great fireships, laden with combustibles, and connected with iron chains, were drawn up in the form of a crescent, floated, in the middle of a dark night, and with a favorable wind, into the bay, and steered against the ships in the New Mole, while three others were directed against other points. Behind them came a long line of row boats and galleys filled with armed men, and these in turn were supported by the heavy ships of the Spanish fleet. The first stage of the enterprise was completely successful, and it was only at one o'clock in the morning that the British sailors became aware, by the sudden glare and explosions, of the danger that was bearing down upon them. With great quickness, daring, and presence of mind, they sprang into their boats, grappled with the burning fireships, towed them clear of the English vessels, and thus not only baffled the design of the enemy, but obtained in the hulks of the captured ships a supply of fuel for which the garrison had urgent need.

The siege was brought to a close only by the general pacification which occurred in 1783. Since then Gibraltar has been left undisturbed in the hands of the English; and it is essentially an English town. A garrison is established there, and martial law prevails, the whole population, both civil and military, being subjected to stringent rules. The gates are shut at sunset, and a gun is fired morning and evening.

When first seen from the sea, the great rock, one thousand four hundred and thirty feet high, seems to rise from under the waves, for the land about it is so low that it appears to have no connection with it. It looks like a lion asleep, with its huge head turned towards Africa.

The *Cristoforo Colon* came to a full stop outside of Algeciras, and small boats were lowered, and others seen putting forth from that small town, which is a straggling little place on the side of the smooth bay opposite Gibraltar.

The Horners were not going to stay at Gibraltar. Two of the party had seen the place, and Miss Lejeune, who was one of them, advised going on to Malaga in the same steamer, to which

THE ROCK OF GIBRALTAR.

Bessie and her father readily agreed. The steamer was to stay several hours at her moorings, and the best thing for the Vaughans to do seemed to be waiting until they should be sent for.

And there was not long to wait, for soon a boat approached the side, rowed by swarthy Spaniards, and bringing a tall gentleman, looking about fifty years old, with a military bearing, and a grave countenance.

Alas! as he came towards them, and they all knew he must be Colonel Vaughan, Miss Lejeune saw at a glance, that his hat was surrounded by black crape. Perhaps Hubert also saw this; perhaps he divined what had happened; for as he darted forward to meet his father, his only word was:

"Mamma?"

There was no way to soften the blow. Colonel Vaughan bent down towards his son, and said in a low tone:

"My dear boy, she is dead. The news came yesterday."

Nana was the only one who began to sob. Miss Lejeune led Bessie and Tommy away, and Mr. Horner withdrew also, to leave the little family alone with their grief.

"I cannot bear it!" cried Bessie. "Aunt Dut, it is terrible."

"Poor Hubert, poor fellow!" said Miss Lejeune, drying her eyes.

They all felt keenly for the Vaughans. All had feared from the accounts of the mother's health, that she could not live; but so soon! they had not anticipated hearing the sad message while they were still together.

"Only yesterday!" said Mr. Horner. "Perhaps while we were so merry coming from Seville."

After a suitable interval, Mr. Horner rejoined the group, and now Colonel Vaughan, with a strong grasp of the hand, thanked him warmly for his kindness to his children.

"I fear I have not expressed myself well in writing," he said. "In fact, I have been almost distracted by my dread — by my knowledge, indeed — of what was to come. I was shocked to learn that the children had left their mother. It was unwise. She might have had the comfort of them, and they" — He could not finish his sentence. Miss Lejeune approached, and without any introduction, said a few words of warm sympathy.

"Papa," said Hubert, "this is Tommy, and this is Bessie Horner."

His father shook hands with both, but Miss Lejeune could not but observe that he took hardly any notice of them.

"Poor man!" she thought; "I dare say he has not given a thought to our party, or wondered once what constituted it. How severely we judged him; and yet one cannot blame him now." Colonel Vaughan, almost as if he had become aware of what was passing in her mind, made an effort to express his gratitude, and some interest in the late adventures of his children.

ROMAN BRIDGE, RONDA.

"I am glad the poor things have had the pleasure of being with you. I am sure they have enjoyed it."

"O, papa, we have!" exclaimed Hubert, his face lighting up. "You cannot imagine what dear, lovely people they are, and how kind they have been!"

He looked round at them all in turn, as if wondering what he should do without these new companions who had become already such old friends.

"I fear that my children have given you some trouble, madam," went on Colonel Vaughan.

Miss Lejeune assured him that, on the contrary, Nana had made the care very light for the rest of them, and then, to cut short these interchanges of compliment, she looked about for Nana. They all saw, then, how the nurse had withdrawn to a seat apart, and was crying bitterly with her face in her hands. Fanny, looking pitiful and bewildered, was holding close to the baby, the only one of the group unconscious of its loss.

"I think we had best be going," said Colonel Vaughan. "We need not detain you longer."

In a short time the parting was over. It was a painful one on all sides. The Vaughans were packed into the small boat, and pulled towards the shore, while the Horners stood watching them from the deck of the steamer, waving handkerchiefs damp with tears. Miss Lejeune was in

SAFETY BOAT.

no mood for sketching. She disappeared below to the ladies' cabin, and it is believed surrendered herself to a good cry.

Before dark the steamer was unloaded and reloaded, her anchor up, and steam, and they were off again, gliding by the immense rock, which stood out in superb relief against a glowing evening sky. After dinner, the small, sad party of Horners gathered close together on deck, for it was cold, and tucked themselves tightly about with wraps and rugs.

As the steamer swept along, new aspects of the rock unfolded themselves, always dark, against the rich background. They could half make out the forms of caves and openings in the base of the cliff, and on top, the flag-staff stood out a fine line against the glow.

The solemn beauty of the evening, and the sad experience of the day, made it a memorable occasion which often came back to them. They talked much of Hubert, and Miss Lejeune told them all he had said of his mother; and they spoke gently and thoughtfully about her death, and of the sweet, strong influence the memory of his mother would have upon the boy, to make him honest, and brave, and true, all his life. Tommy was silent throughout. His heart was full of sorrow.

It was much later than his usual bed-time when they all withdrew together for the night. For some reason, there were no separate staterooms to be had, and Bessie and Miss Lejeune therefore shared the general ladies' cabin, with a Spanish lady who had a wonderful coiffure, in which she lay down that night and rose the next morning.

Just as he was going to sleep, Mr. Horner was roused by Tommy's voice, in a berth above him.

"Papa!"

"Well!"

"You did not see the monkeys!"

"You are another," growled his parent; "go to sleep."

Hubert had described, for all English boys have heard of, the monkeys who live on the Rock. They are protected by strict laws, and are much talked of, but seldom seen, inhabiting the higher and eastern part, unless they are driven down by cold winds. There is a myth that their ancestors came over from Africa in days when an isthmus, instead of a strait, was between the two countries; a theory not impossible to entertain.

CHAPTER XXV.

MALAGA.

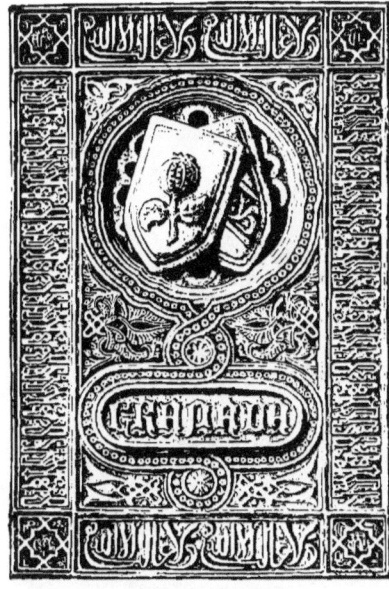
ARMS OF GRANADA.

BESSIE was awake at dawn, and looked out of the little round port-hole, as well as she could, which was close by her head, in the hot, stuffy berth of the ladies' cabin. The Andalusian lady was still asleep in a berth below, and so was Miss Lejeune, and there was no occasion for stirring yet; but they must have reached Malaga, for the ship was at rest, though not quiet. Men were trampling about overhead, tumbling heavy barrows, and delighting, apparently, in all those noises least soothing to sleepers below.

Bessie climbed softly down from her high perch, and as she had slept in her boots, in a very few minutes was ready to go up on deck, where for half an hour she had to herself a lovely scene; the glowing day coming slowly into the sky, and pouring its light over the town, which was close at hand, for the steamer was tied up to the pier.

When the party was assembled, they left the boat, and walked across the Alameda to the hotel, baggage following, and were before long established in comfortable rooms, with baths and breakfast to follow.

They were not in good condition for enjoying the sights of Malaga. The sad scene of the day before was still fresh upon their hearts. Tommy, especially, missed his companion, and every moment reminded him of the poor little fellow, and his forlorn face at parting. Miss Lejeune reported that she had passed a vile night on the *Cristoforo Colon*, and Mr. Horner was always somewhat knocked up by sea excursions, while Bessie was by ten o'clock as sleepy as a cat, after her early ascent upon deck.

THE CATHEDRAL AND PORT OF MALAGA.

As they were loitering over coffee at that hour,— for they had not succeeded in getting it sooner,— Miss Lejeune said:

"Why do we go on to Granada to-day? We do not feel like going out now to see the town. We might all try the very attractive beds which I have been regarding with longing, and see Malaga by and by, in the cool part of the day."

"Very good," said Mr. Horner; "the only reason for pressing on is,— letters."

"Yes, letters! It is an age since we have had any. Still, it will make only one day's difference."

"Do stay, papa, I am so sleepy!" said Bessie.

So they stayed over twenty-four hours at Malaga, which they

BANKS OF THE DARRO.

had not intended to do, thinking it not an especially attractive town. They found, however, interesting pictures in the cathedral, and in the hospitable private house of an American gentleman, living in Malaga, the most beautiful Alonzo Cano they had seen. Miss Lejeune was delighted with it; it fulfilled all her desire to give this painter a high place among the Spanish masters.

The Alameda, or shady walk, is long and wide, with a handsome fountain, said to have been ordered by Charles the Fifth, the Emperor, for his palace at Granada, then seized by Barbarossa, but afterward regained by the Spaniards.

"How do you feel, Bessie," said her father, as they were strolling along under the trees of the Alameda, "at hearing of your Barbarossa down here?"

"Is it not wonderful," she replied, "when we thought we left him sound asleep in his cavern, waiting for the ravens to cease to fly around the mountain. But," she added, "I cannot be thinking of German Emperors now. Only think, papa, to-morrow we shall be in Granada, and need attend to nothing but our dear Moors."

In fact, after the Horners had reached Granada, and were established in the Washington Irving Hotel, all their previous impressions of Spain grew pale before the charm of the life they were now beginning upon.

It was June; the weather was lovely: the roses and pomegranates and jasmines were in perfection of bloom, perfuming the air, nightingales were singing everywhere, and the sound of fountains and falling water made a running accompaniment to their music; in short, everything was in harmony with the romance of the Alhambra.

North of Granada rises a long ridge of rocky land between two rivers, the Darro and Xenil; the ridge slopes downwards towards the town, intersected by a long avenue of elm-trees, but spreading out near the top into two tablelands, or broad terraces, bordered by steep ravines. On the western terrace stands the Alhambra, its base washed by the Darro. On the eastern one stand the Vermilion Towers, beyond which the land slopes more gently down into the precincts of the town of Granada. These two terraces were formerly girt with walls and towers, and connected together

PUERTA DEL VINO.

with winding lanes; and within the circuit thus fortified, stood the palaces and villas of the Caliphs of Granada, as well as their chief fortresses; so many that the enclosure was called a city. There were other villas and palaces in the neighborhood, but the Hadhira, or court of the Caliphs, on the western plateau, and within the walls, constituted the Alhambra proper. The walls and their enclosure occupy the greater part of this terrace; but there is some level ground outside, and this has been availed of for two hotels, facing each other upon the road which leads to the grand gate of entrance — the Siete Suelos, and the Washington Irving. Nothing could be more charming then their situation, in the leafy avenue, planted by tall elms, surrounded by their own gardens and those of neighboring villas, overlooking, on one side, the crumbling orange-colored walls of the Alhambra, and on the other a view extending to the snowy slopes of the Sierra . Nevada. There is but little to choose between the two hotels; at present, they are both well kept; the Horners were advised, in Malaga, to take the Washington Irving, and a sort of loyalty, as Americans, to the name, perhaps influenced them in the decision. They had excellent rooms in an angle commanding all the different views possible. A pleasant English family were established in the house; opposite, at the Sieta Suelos, a gay party of artists were coming and going, and in the evenings they sat before the door, striking the guitar and singing Malagueñas. This, then, was the culmination of the Spanish tour; with everything so enchanting around them, the Horners were content to let the time slip by as it would, seeing and enjoying all, without haste, but not without rest. The grounds are open to all, to wander about at will, and friendly guides are at hand to conduct and explain.

First of all, after they had arrived and seen how delightful it was, came their thirst for letters; and Mr. Horner and Tommy walked down into the town, along the steep, broad, shaded road, which reminded them not a little of the descent from Heidelberg Castle. They returned in several hours, hot, and out of breath with coming fast up the height, in their desire to share the big budget from America and Luz, which had been accumulating at the banker's. Again good news; everything right on both sides of the Atlantic; the Pyrénées party still without events, but happy.

"I am so glad mamma keeps perfectly well!" said Bessie. This sentence betrayed a thought that had possessed them all secretly since hearing the death of Mrs. Vaughan; a vague dread that something might be wrong with their own dear ones.

"The usual amount of engagements and marriages in America," remarked Miss Lejeune, looking up from her letters.

"You always say that, aunt Dut," said Tommy, who, having received no letters of his own, was hanging round to pick up intelligence from the rest, while they, each completely absorbed in his or her own budget, paid but little attention to the exclamations of the others.

"Mary has had a telegram from Mr. Hervey, to say he had reached New York!" cried Bessie.

"Extravagant man!" said Miss Lejeune, putting down her letter.

"Only two words, which they had agreed upon to mean all right," went on Bessie. "She don't say what they were!"

"Well, well," remarked Miss Lejeune, and once more continued, as she fumbled with the sheets of the correspondence, "well, well!"

GYPSY GIRL

The windows were opened and the air fluttered lightly about the room. A dish of great oranges stood on the table, with which Tommy was filling up his time and stomach. A bunch of orange blossoms, and some full-blown roses, were tumbling about in a goblet where Bessie had hastily thrust them, as she came in, hearing the good news that letters had arrived. All Miss Lejeune's sketching materials were lying on a chair where she too had dropped them when Mr. Horner came in. Her sketch was spoiled, for the orange colored wash over the turrets of the Siete Suelos would dry before she could finish it. No matter; that was nothing, since they had such good news.

Bessie finished her letters and went to the window.

"Let us send for mamma and Mary, and then stay here forever!" she said. "I see no reason for going further."

"And Phil," said Tommy.

"Of course I mean Phil! Come here, Tommy, and look down at this gypsy!"

Their rooms were in the third story, so that they overlooked the narrow terrace garden belonging to the hotel. They saw a girl dressed in all the picturesque garments of a Spanish gypsy, standing with a jug poised on her head in an attitude for a model, while a young lady was rapidly sketching her in charcoal. The artist was surrounded by several small children watching her work. The gypsy beamed all over her face, with vanity and satisfaction, evidently thinking that her personal charms had recommended her.

Tommy said softly, "I do believe that is the American girl we saw at Irun with all the bags and umbrellas."

"Where can she have been since!" exclaimed Bessie; "and where are the rest?"

As the Horners were entering the pleasant dining-room for almuerzo, the whole force of waiters and maids were engaged in speeding the parting of some people who were being packed into an open carriage with their numerous belongings.

"It is the other H's!" cried Miss Lejeune.

CHAPTER XXVI.

THE CONQUEST OF GRANADA.

AFTER the middle of the thirteenth century, the constantly contracting circle of Moorish dominion in Spain shrank into the narrow limits of the province of Granada. Yet on this comparatively small point of their ancient domain, the Saracens erected a new kingdom of sufficient strength to resist for more than two centuries, the united forces of the Spanish monarchies.

The Moorish territory of Granada contained within a circuit of about one hundred and eighty leagues, all the physical resources of a great empire. Its broad valleys were intersected by mountains rich in mineral wealth, occupied by a robust and hardy population. Its pastures were fed by abundant streams, and its coasts commanded the commerce of the Mediterranean. In the midst, crowning the whole, rose the beautiful city of Granada. In the days of the Moors it was encompassed by a wall flanked by a thousand and thirty towers; and above it rose the fortress of the Alhambra, whose magnificent ruins still manifest the taste, opulence, and luxury of its proprietors. The streets are represented to have been narrow, the houses lofty, with turrets of curiously wrought larch or marble, and with cornices of shining metal, that glittered like stars through the dark foliage of the orange groves; the whole is compared to "an enamelled vase, sparkling with hyacinths and emeralds," in the florid strains of Arabic writers, describing the glories of Granada.

At the foot of this Aladdin's palace, lies the cultivated plain called the *vega*, so celebrated as the arena for more than two centuries of the contests between Moor and Christian. The Arabs

GATE OF JUSTICE, ALHAMBRA.

expended upon it all their knowledge of cultivation. The waters of the Xenil flowed through it in a thousand channels, for its perfect irrigation. A constant succession of fruits and crops was obtained throughout the year. Products of opposite latitudes were transplanted there with success. The hemp of the North flourished in the shadow of the vine and the olive. The seaports swarmed with traders from Europe, Africa, and the Levant, so that "Granada became the common city of all nations." Such was the reputation of its citizens, that "their bare word was more relied upon than a written contract is now among us," as a Spanish writer says.

The sovereigns of Granada were often distinguished by liberal tastes, and they loved above all the display of a princely pomp. Each day presented a succession of fêtes and tournaments, in which the knights displayed their horsemanship and their skill in the feats peculiar to their nation. Life was with them a long carnival; but the people were diligent, industrious, and honest.

FERDINAND AND ISABELLA.

The Moorish and Christian knights were in the habit of exchanging visits at their respective courts, for the Spaniards had been gradually rising in civilization to the level of their enemies, and the two races were now upon a footing of equality, and even friendship; and thus the Spanish Arabs were distinguished by the same qualities as the Christian knights.

This combination of Oriental magnificence and knightly prowess served to soften the defects common to Mohammedan institutions, and enabled the reign of the Moors to hold out against the Christian arms for so long a time. Moreover, its strength lay less in its own resources, than in the weakness of its enemies, who, after the death of Saint Ferdinand, in the thirteenth century, became more and more divided by quarrels amongst themselves. But the union of all the provinces by the marriage of Ferdinand and Isabella, put an end for the time to such dissensions. No sooner had these sovereigns restored internal tranquility to their dominions, and made the strength effective which had been acquired by their union under one government, than they turned their eyes upon that part of Spain over which the crescent had reigned for nearly eight centuries. Amicable relations were existing between the Christian princes, and the rulers of Granada, until 1466, when the Caliph, who at that time succeeded to the throne, resisted the payment of the annual tribute imposed on his predecessors, proudly saying that "the mints of Granada coined no longer gold, but steel."

The storm burst upon a small town called Zahara, which was surprised one night by this Moorish monarch, Muley Abul Hacen; who, scaling the walls under the favor of a furious tempest, swept away the whole population of the place,— men, women and children,— in slavery to Granada.

The Spaniards soon retaliated by seizing the ancient city of Alhama, famous for its baths, and the favorite resort of the monarchs of Granada, embellished with all the magnificence of a royal residence. This first conquest by the Christians was achieved with a gallantry and daring unsurpassed by any other during the war. The report of the disaster fell like the knell of their own doom upon the Moors.

> Ay de mi, Alhama —
> Woe is me, Alhama —

is the burden of the melancholy ballad about it. But the intelligence spread satisfaction throughout Castile, and was especially agreeable to the sovereigns. After learning the news, a chronicler of the time says, "During all the while he sat at dinner the prudent Ferdinand was working in his mind the course best to be adopted."

The Moors now besieged Alhama in their turn, and for more than three weeks it was in peril; but the monarch alarmed by seeing Christian reinforcements, broke up his encampment and retreated to his capital; and although he made another attempt to regain it, the Christians took possession of the city, and entered it with great ceremony. The mosques were purified and consecrated as Christian temples. Isabella, the queen, presented bells, crosses and sumptuous plate to show that she entered into the war through zeal for the true faith. The army was enlarged, and she caused a fleet to be manned, to sweep the Mediterranean as far as the Straits of Gibraltar.

Thus the struggle went on with many feats of daring and bravery on both sides. The names of the heroes who fought in this prolonged contest are among the most famous warriors of all time.

Division among the Moors did more for the Christians than any successes of their own; quarrels between the women of the Alhambra led to a war in the streets of Granada. One of the wives of Abul Hacen lowered her son in a basket from a tower of the Alhambra, to save him from the jealousy of another sultana. This was the beginning. Later, the father was expelled from his own capital. He sought refuge in Malaga, which still adhered to him, with some other places of importance, while Granada, and by far the larger part of the kingdom, proclaimed the authority of the boy who escaped in the basket — Abu Abdallah, or Boabdil, as he is usually called.

He was surnamed, by the Spanish writers, "*El Chico*," the Little, — to distinguish him from another Boabdil, his uncle, — and "*El Zogoybi*," the Unfortunate, by the Moors, as the last of his race destined to wear the crown of Granada. The foolish ambition of the sultana, his mother, not only destroyed the future of the son she quarrelled for, but brought ruin upon the Moorish dynasty.

Thus the war went on, and much blood was shed on both sides. Isabella was the soul of the contest. She sometimes visited the camp in person, encouraging the soldiers with gifts of clothes and money. She followed the army from place to place, and was with the camp in the spring of 1491, when the Spanish army finally sat down before Granada, not more than six miles from the city. It is said that one night about the middle of July, the drapery of Isabella's tent took fire, and was not extinguished until several

MOORISH ARCHES.

of the neighboring ones had been consumed. The queen and everybody else escaped unhurt; but the accident caused Isabella to determine upon building a safer town, which was finished in less than three months It was called Santa Fé.

DOS HERMANAS, ALHAMBRA.

There is a pretty anecdote of Gonsalvo of Cordova, the Gran Capitan, connected with this event, which relates that when he learned how the fire had consumed the royal tent, with the greater part of the queen's clothing, he supplied the queen so amply from the splendid wardrobe of his wife, as led Isabella to say that the fire had done more execution in his castle than in her own quarters.

Every one has read the story of the surrender, in Washington Irving's *Conquest of Granada*. The besieged city was suffering the distress of famine. Autumn arrived, a rigorous winter was approaching; the people sank into deep despondency. They remembered that Boabdil had been pronounced unfortunate at his birth, and they recalled that the fall of Granada had been foretold at the time of the capture of Zahara. The councillors of the monarch said "Surrender!" they declared that the people could no longer support their sufferings.

Boabdil el Chico yielded to the general voice.

"*Allah achbar!* God is great," he said. "It is in vain to struggle against the will of Heaven."

The capitulation for the surrender was signed on the twenty-fifth of November, 1481.

"It was a night of doleful lamentings within the walls of the Alhambra, for the household of Boabdil were preparing to take a last farewell of that delightful abode. Before the dawn of day, a mournful cavalcade moved obscurely out of a postern gate of the Alhambra, and departed through one of the most retired quarters of the city. The mother of Boabdil rode on in silence, with dejected, yet dignified demeanor; but his wife and all the household gave way to loud lamentations as they gave a last look at the mass of gloomy towers behind them. At a hamlet at some distance from the city, they waited until they should be joined by the king.

"At dawn the Christian camp was in motion, and a body of distinguished cavaliers proceeded to take possession of the Alhambra. The Moorish king came forth from the gate to deliver up the palace. He passed mournfully on along the same road by which the cavaliers had come, descending to the Vega to meet the Catholic sovereigns. The troops entered the Alhambra, the gates

ARABESQUE, IN THE ALHAMBRA.

of which were wide open, and all its splendid courts and halls silent and deserted.

"The sovereigns waited below with impatience. At length they saw the silver cross elevated on the Torre de la Vela, and beside it was planted the pennon of the glorious apostle St. James." * * *

Having surrendered the keys to the sovereigns, the unfortunate Boabdil joined his family. At two leagues distance the cavalcade ascended an eminence commanding the last view of Granada. As they arrived at this spot, the Moors paused to take a farewell gaze at their beloved city. Never had it appeared so lovely in their eyes. While they yet looked, a light cloud of smoke burst forth from the citadel, and presently a peal of artillery, faintly heard, told that the city was taken.

The heart of Boabdil could no longer contain itself.

"*Allah achbar!* God is great," he said; but he burst into tears.

His mother, indignant, said:

"You do well to weep like a woman for what you failed to defend like a man."

The point of view commanding the last prospect of Granada, is known as *El ultimo suspiro del Moro;* or, the last sigh of the Moor.

CHAPTER XXVII.

THE ALHAMBRA.

UNDER the Moors, the Alhambra was the scene of many romantic events, the legends connected with which still people its courts with phantoms.

The road leading up from the hotel to the entrance is shaded with tall trees, and water trickles down the side making the

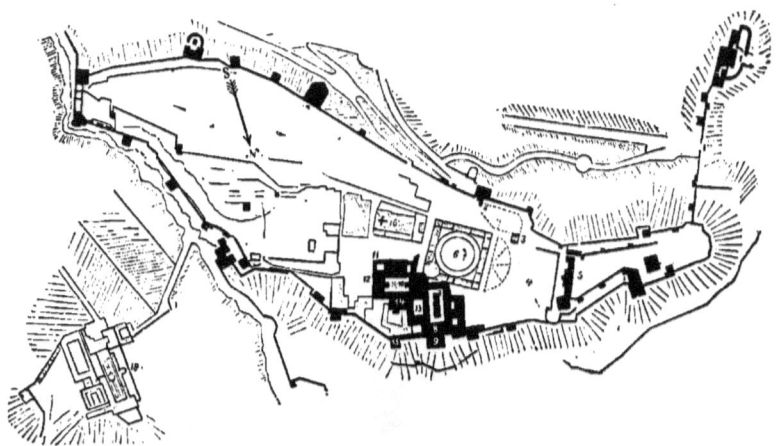

PLAN OF THE ALHAMBRA.

grass fresh and green. The walls are of a beautiful red or orange color, which is shared by the soil; this alone gives a glowing aspect to the scene. The chief place of entrance (2 on the plan) is called the Gate of Justice. It is more than a gate, being a square tower, the upper part of which contains rooms where people live. Their little flower pots filled with bright blossoms, stand on the ledge of the window. The horseshoe arch of entrance is below; for as the ground is terraced, the level of the palace is above that of the arch, and is approached by an ascent, and a staircase within the tower.

Over this arch there is carved an outstretched hand pointing upward, to avert the evil eye; over the second one a key is sculptured; a symbol of the power of the prophet to open and shut the gates of heaven. The passages within the tower wind about under several arches, until they lead out and up to the walled-in plateau, on which the Alhambra stands. A little farther on is another gateway, and building, called the Puerto del Vino (3); it formerly contained a Mihràb, or Moorish chapel.

From the high terrace near these two gates, is a lovely view across the deep ravine to the Sierra Nevada, always slightly touched with snow, and taking on beautiful lights, according to the time of day; dark blue in the morning, and, as evening approaches, roseate; for in addition to the sunset tints, the natural color of the soil and stone make the tone of the range warm and rich. Here opens a large plaza, called the Place of the Cisterns, on one side of which is the Alcazaba, or fortress, with its dismantled castle (5), while opposite it appears the palace of Charles the Fifth (6), which he began to build, but never finished. He destroyed the greater part of the beautiful winter palace of the Moors, to make room for his own, and afterward abandoned his plan, leaving the unfinished ruin, with open arches, staring to the sky. It is said that earthquakes discouraged him from going on with his palace. There are planted garden beds, and walks leading along the side of it, to a plain, unadorned wall, through which a door leads to the real glories of the Alhambra.

Here found themselves one morning, Mr. Horner and Miss Lejeune, Bessie and Tommy; Bessie grumbling, as usual, at Charles the Fifth, and Ferdinand and Isabella, who have left their traces so often in the destruction of Moorish ornament.

"I do believe," said Bessie, "that Isabella herself rode on a whitewash brush!"

COURT OF MYRTLES.

"Perhaps she was the old woman —

Old woman, said I,
To sweep the cobwebs from the sky!"

said Tommy.

They passed on through the gate. Charles the Fifth and Isabella were forgotten. The transition was magical; they felt at once transported into other times, and were treading the scenes of the *Arabian Nights*. They were in the Court of Myrtles, a long, open patio (7), of which the floor is taken up by an immense basin, more than a hundred feet long, bordered by myrtle-trees and roses. It is surrounded by a light arcade of Moorish columns, and at the upper end rises the great Tower of Comares. (8) The pillars here and elsewhere are of extreme lightness, and the or-

COURT OF LIONS.

namentation of the capital varies in each; slender arches spring from the capitals, and bend gracefully till they meet. A dado of azulejos, or colored tiles, runs along the wall, from the floor, of brightest colors, with great variety of patterns. The eye is never tired of following these designs, nor those of the arabesque work above, into which are woven Arabic sentences, in the graceful lettering of that language. Across the water is seen the vista made by the entrance to the Hall of Ambassadors (9), the chief room of the Tower of Comares. The tower and its colonnades are reflected in the clear still water of the pool.

"Oh, how lovely!" exclaimed Miss Lejeune. "This surpasses all my dreams of it."

"Let us stay here, and not go any further to-day!" said Bessie.

Tommy was well content to study the goldfish in the clear water, rather startled, as he leaned over, to catch the perfect reflection of his own face on the surface of the pool, with behind it an intensely blue sky studded with woolly white clouds. He looked up instinctively, and saw above the graceful fretwork of the court, the real bright sky and clouds, just like the mirrored ones.

"Our guide apparently expects us to move on," remarked Mr. Horner. "We can let him gallop us through once, and then come at our leisure as often as we like."

"Not gallop us, papa," said Bessie, taking hold of his hand; "a quiet little trot will satisfy him."

They were led into the Court of Lions (10), where Bessie was at once in love with the somewhat clumsy animals of Arab origin, that form the group of the fountain in the centre.

"I must embrace this one!" she cried, and did so, to Tommy's disgust and mortification. He looked round to see if there were any observers.

These lions must not be looked at as efforts of sculpture to represent accurately the king of beasts, but as emblems of strength and courage. They are of white marble, with manes like the scales of a griffin, and water comes from their mouths.

The hall of the Abencerrages (11) leads from the Court of Lions.

Its name comes from the legend that Boabdil, the last king of Granada, invited the chiefs of this line to a banquet, and had them taken out, one by one, after the feast, through a small wicket, to the fountain of the Court of Lions, where they were beheaded; a massacre which contributed to his ruin, as they were the main support of his kingdom, and had helped to put him on his throne. The stains of their blood are still pointed out.

"Does not that shake your faith in Boabdil, Bessie?" asked her father, when they were listening to this tale of the guide.

"I do not believe a word of it!" said Bessie indignantly. "Boabdil would not have been such a fool, and I have great doubts as to the existence of the Abencerrages!"

The guide, however, to enforce the story, told how there was often heard at night, in the Court of Lions, a low, confused murmur, with the distant clanking of chains.

The Abencerrages were a family or faction said to hold a prominent position in the Moorish kingdom of Granada in the thirteenth century. The name appears to have been derived from one Yussuf ben Serragh, the head of the tribe in the time of Mohammed the Seventh, who did that sovereign good service in his struggles to retain the crown of which he was three times deprived. Nothing is known of the family with certainty, but the name is familiar in romance.

On the opposite side of the Court is the Hall of the Two Sisters (14), paved with white marble and beautifully incrusted with tiles. It leads to the Mirador of Lindaraxa, a smaller room, containing a window with a double Moorish arch which opens upon a patio full of orange-trees. The bright sunlight glanced upon the ripe fruit and shining leaves without, and the arabesque work framed the scene like a picture. This was one of the women's apartments. The name is from two marble slabs of equal size in the pavement, which are called the Two Sisters.

Another room leading from the Court of Lions (12) contained some strange pictures, painted on the ceiling, which interested both Bessie and Miss Lejeune. It is a question how they come to be

WINDOW IN HALL OF AMBASSADORS.

there, and who painted them, for the Moors were forbidden by the Koran to represent living subjects. A French writer imagines that John Van Eyck went to the Alhambra in 1428, and that he painted for the Moorish kings. The subjects are singular, and hard to make out, especially as they could only be seen in a very uncomfortable position for the head.

Bessie liked to imagine that a Caliph had employed some great Christian artist to come and paint for him; perhaps even a Bellini, from Venice; but Miss Lejeune pronounced the work to be of later date, and more likely after the conquest of the Moors.

The two stayed so long that they found themselves alone, and hastened to regain the others, who had retraced their steps through the Myrtle Court to the Hall of the Ambassadors.

This is the largest in the Alhambra, and occupies all the Tower of Comares. It is a great square room, high to the centre of the dome. It was the grand reception room, and the throne of the Caliph was placed opposite the entrance. Now, like all the other rooms, it is bare; the imagination has to furnish them all with thrones, divans, and rich couches and cushions, as well as with little feminine trifles for the niches, such as vases, and trinkets.

The walls are so thick that the windows make deep recesses, from which are lovely views across the Vega, and towards the other buildings of the enclosure. It is from one of these windows that Ayeshah, the mother of Boabdil, is said to have lowered him in a basket to save his life.

The little group stood in the middle of the hall, listening to the guide's explanations. When he turned, however, to lead them further, Bessie sat resolutely down in the embrasure of a window, saying:

"I can no more! I have seen enough for one time; my head is bewildered, my legs are tired,"—

"And you are hungry!" finished her father, taking out his watch. "I suspect that is the case with all of us, and that we have done enough for once. Ah, yes; high noon, and high time for almuerzo."

And so they explained their wishes to the guide, who, accustomed to driving a swarm of visitors before him, as flies are urged on by a whisk, was amazed, and fancied they were bored; he began a sort of an apology for the nature of the entertainment.

"It is because we enjoy it so much that we want to keep the rest for another time," said Miss Lejeune, in elegant Castilian. Either the Castilian, or the sentiment, was not fully understood by the man, who still appeared downcast; but he understood a peseta which Mr. Horner put in his hand, and consented to show them the shortest way out.

The sun glared bright on the plaza, but the shady road outside the walls was cool and perfumed, and a few steps brought them to the hotel.

CHAPTER XXVIII.

MORE OF THE ALHAMBRA.

THE ground the Horners had been over that morning included the greater part of the palace of the Alhambra; there was still left the suite of rooms devoted to the bath by the Moorish possessors of the place (13). It contains preparations for every luxury connected with bathing; raised niches for couches, with cushions, fountains, balconies for music, which they enjoyed after the bath, and baths themselves, of white marble.

Day after day the Horners visited the palace. It became their habit to meet in the Court of Lions after their sketching or exploring in other places was over. There was nothing to prevent Bessie from wandering by herself all over the pile of buildings, and this she greatly enjoyed, though sometimes a little puzzled by the windings she discovered in the lower regions, underneath the Tower of Comares, where there are some long dark passages. She loved to sit in the small garden of Linderaxa, shut in on all sides by columns and walls. It is full of orange-trees, the same that are seen from the Mirador of Linderaxa, and in the middle of them is a fountain. Here she liked to bring Irving's *Alhambra;* it was just the place to read his legends of its first inhabitants. She only wished that he had recorded, or invented, more of them; for every nook suggests a mystery. Who was Linderaxa for whom the beautiful mirador was named, and who used to wander in the little garden, and what was her fate? Did she live and die happy, or did she pine away?

Bessie envied the experiences of Mr. Irving, who lived in rooms actually within the palace precincts. He had the place all to himself, and learned to know it before the great band of tourists had invaded the spot, or guide-books, with their convenient gossip, laid bare the secrets of the Alhambra. But she had the consolation of knowing that it is now in far better condition than in Irving's time.

Early in the century, the Alhambra was in a state of ruin, from neglect. The governor's wife kept her donkey in the chapel, and used one of the patios for a sheep-pen. Afterwards the place was turned into barracks, and the blue and white pavements of the courts were torn up. The French, in 1812, ruined the towers and blew up several of them, among others the beautiful Siete Suelos, in order that the Alhambra might be useless thereafter as a fortress, and carried off all that was portable within the walls.

In those days the Court of Lions was encumbered with rubbish. The animals were tumbled down on the ground. It was a woman named Tia Antonia, described by Irving, who restored it. She was permitted to make a living by showing the gardens, and she set the lions on their legs, cleared away the rubbish, and did her best to make improvements. In spite of her efforts, and some trifling restorations by authorities, neglect ruled. Several

ENTRANCE TO HALL OF AMBASSADORS.

slight earthquakes added to the ruin. At length, in 1862, Queen Isabella the Second, mother of the present king, who was herself then on the throne, made a visit to Granada, and shocked, we may suppose, at the discreditable condition of the greatest glory of her kingdom, she commissioned Señor Contreras, a gentleman of learning and ability, to repair the palace of the Moorish kings, beginning at her own expense. He lives on the spot, and is still at work, gradually restoring here and there, with great taste and judgment, the different halls, reproducing the original design where it was lost, but never making new innovations. His work has the fault, perhaps, of looking too fresh and modern, but this cannot be avoided; and there is so much of the old left that the two help each other, and work together to give a true impression of the ancient Alhambra.

Another of Bessie's favorite retreats was the Mirador de la Reina (15), which is reached by a long corridor from the Hall of Ambassadors. It contains the prettiest little tocador imaginable, with arched windows on all sides, as open as a summer house, with superb views; for here the bluff is very steep, and falls off to the valley of the river. *Tocador* means dressing-room; the guide called it in his rudimentary English, "combing-house," and Bessie and Tommy always spoke of it as the combing-house. It is not more than nine feet square; in one corner is a marble slab drilled with holes, through which perfumes used to be wafted up from below during the toilet of the sultana.

This pretty little place is said to have been refitted by Italian artists in the early part of the last century, when Philip the Fifth, the Bourbon, brought his queen, Isabella of Parma, to the Alhambra. This brilliant royal party brought back a transient gayety and loveliness to the scene; since then its courts have been silent and deserted by royalty.

From the narrow balcony which surrounds the combing-house, the palace and gardens of the Generalife are seen. Between them and the Alhambra is a narrow gorge. The children found that by scrambling down from a gate below the tower of Comares, they reached a path leading along the walls on the outside quite around the fortifications, by which they could regain the road leading down from the Generalife to their hotel. The path was rough, and furrowed by channels, where, in rainy weather, streams

EL MIRADOR DE LA REINA.

must pour through. It was chiefly frequented by gypsies passing up from their quarter, flocks of sheep, or little parties of donkeys; but the steep sides of the gorge were sprinkled with wild flowers, and the yellow red walls of the fortress rose high, with here and there a square tower, overshadowed by trees growing within the enclosure, which at this end is a deserted, uncultivated field overrun with weeds, though pomegranates struggle up uncared for, covered with their gorgeous scarlet blossoms. One of these square towers is the *Torre de las*

Infantas, once the residence of Moorish princesses, and the scene of Irving's pretty tale about Zohra, Zorayda, and Zorahayda. Señor Contreras has recently been restoring its mosaics, arabesques, and azulejos. He has made a spick and span new little Moorish retreat of it, which might make one long to be a Moorish princess, with all the modern improvements.

An arch over the children's favorite path, built by Charles the Fifth, is modern, and has not the Moorish curve. It is now overgrown with ivy, and is crumbling in parts, so that it has as much the air of antiquity as the rest. It is said that Charles the Fifth abandoned his palace on account of the earthquakes which visited it from time to time.

"Those earthquakes that frightened Charles the Fifth, were only Boabdil shaking the ground from beneath," said Bessie, "to drive him off. When the Moors return, they do not wish to find Christian architecture usurping the place of their palaces."

The legend says that when the Moors were driven out of Granada, only phantoms vanished in ships over the sea to Morocco. The real ones were swallowed up in the mountain upon which the Alhambra stands, and there they sit, in silent state, awaiting the restoration of their kingdom.

"Is it not comforting to think of them down there now?" said Bessie.

"Is there any telephonic communication, do you think, between them and Barbarossa in his mountain?" asked her father.

"Communication, but not telephonic," replied Bessie, readily accepting his question. "The ravens carry messages to the storks, and so they hear twice a year, when the storks pass over and back. It is not so swift as the telegraph, but they hear often enough, as there is nothing much to tell."

The Siete Suelos, one of the prettiest bits of ruin, has its legend also, according to which, underneath it sit two Moors guarding a heavy coffer full of Arabic coins and rich jewels. This tower, as has been said, is just opposite or behind the two hotels. The other little towers (17, etc.) upon the battlements, are in process of restoration by Señor Contreras, and contain the same beautiful arabesque and mosaics.

The favorite resort at sunset is the Torre de la Vela, reached by passing through the gateway of the Alcazaba (5), and along a brick-laid garden walk upon the lofty terrace called the Adarves, laid out upon the line of bastions; a sheer descent into the valley below. This narrow terrace is planted with roses, jasamine, magnolia, and all manner of garden flowers. The platform at the foot of the Torre de la Vela is a mass of brilliant geraniums; many vines, one with pale blue blossoms, cling to the walls.

The panorama from the top of this tower is glorious. Below lies Granada, and beyond it stretches the vega, thirty miles in extent, and hemmed in by a wall of mountains in every direction. It is scattered over with villages; every foot of its soil has its battle and its ballad.

The Torre de la Vela, or Watch Tower, is so called because here hangs a bell intended to be struck once every five minutes, from nine in the evening until four in the morning. The bell is also rung on the second of January, the anniversary of the day, 1492, when the Christian flag was first unfurled by Cardinal Mendoza, after the surrender of Granada.

At sunset the snowy tops of the Sierra glow with warm tints; darkness slowly creeps over the plain, and if the moon is full, the effect is wonderful. One evening, careless of dinner, our party lingered to watch the fading of daylight, and afterwards went back to the Court of Lions, to get the effect of moonlight among the arches of the Alhambra. They had to wait a long time for the moon to be high enough in the heavens to throw any light down upon the courts. The darkness was vague and mysterious. They sat upon the low steps of the courtyard, leaning against the slender pillars; talked in low voices, of the Moors, and their shadows, which might be moving about them.

Suddenly a shaft of light shot across the patio. The moon had climbed the wall, and soon its yellow light flooded the opening, and made sharp-cut shadows upon the pavement.

CHAPTER XXIX.

THE GENERALIFE.

DURING the rest of their stay, the Horners felt very learned as to the situation of the different places of interest about the Alhambra, and could find their way about without any guide. They had procured a general permission to wander over the gardens of the Generalife, and here soon Bessie and Tommy established a habit of spending the morning. Tommy missed Hubert so much, that his usual high spirits forsook him for a time; instead of forming his own plans, and disappearing from the family to carry them out, as he used to when Hubert was on hand to share them, he stuck close to Bessie, who, indeed, was very glad of the change from Fanny Vaughan, who had proved a dull and listless child, to Tom, always wide awake, and an entertaining companion. The brother and sister, in fact, were now becoming intimate for the first time; for Tom had taken the sudden jump from a little boy, petted and laughed at, to a manly fellow with opinions to be respected. The absence of Philip, like taking a weight off a growing plant, made him shoot up independently. He was already almost as tall as Bessie.

A road from the Siete Suelos, turning off near the beautiful arch of Charles the Fifth, leads to the palace and gardens of the Generalife. They belong to the Marquis of Campotejar, better known as one of the Grimaldi Pallavicini of Genoa, a Moorish race, descended from an uncle of Boabdil, Cidi Aya, who became a Christian, and was then called Don Pedro; to him the Generalife was given at the time of the conquest of Granada. Thus it is that Boabdil's sword is in the possession of the family.

Probably none of the present members of it have ever seen their lovely estate in Granada. They possess several splendid palaces in Italy, but none can rival, for romantic association and lofty position, their Spanish castle.

The long garden walks are lined with oleanders, tall cypress-trees, and hedges of myrtle. Through these the entrance is reached, a door in a blank wall, which leads into a patio with a garden, through which a canal flows under evergreen arches, formed by yews twisted and cut into odd patterns. A long gallery with slender pillars and arches runs along the left, from which the Alhambra is seen, close at hand, across the deep ravine. The gardens of the Generalife are a series of terraces. By broad steps, one plateau after another is reached, up to the highest point where a mirador crowns the slopes. The view is very wide. The whole ground-plan of the Alhambra fortress can here best be seen and understood, and the marvellous range of the snow-capped Sierra Nevada. The Court of Cypresses forms a part of one of the terraces. It is square, with a pond in the centre, surrounded by hedges of roses, and a row of immensely tall cypresses, one of them called the Cypress of the Sultana; said to have been two centuries old in the time of Boabdil. The trellised grapevines also date back to the time of the Moorish kings, as their stems, thick like a tree, readily suggest.

In the house the ornamentation is almost hidden by whitewash. There are some pictures in the principal hall, interesting historically, not as works of art. Among them hangs the portrait of Boabdil, el Rey Chico, with a fair face and gentle expression. Bessie looked long at this picture every time she entered the place. His uncle is much fiercer looking, from whom the present proprietor is descended. Ferdinand and Isabella are there, and Gonsalvo, the Gran Capitan.

From this mirador a little gate opens upon the wild hillside, and the children often scrambled up, still higher, to the Silla del Moro. It is but a stone's throw, and there is a kind of path. The view is magnificent; straight down the valley of the Darro, apparently uninhabited, but in reality peopled with gypsies. They live in

CYPRESS WALK IN THE GENERALIFE.

caves underground, and nothing is visible of their populous suburb but a luxurious jungle of prickly pears and other shrubs.

The odd name Generalife is Arabic, and means "the garden of the architect."

Only one portion of the Alhambra now remained unexplored — the Torres Vermejas, or Vermilion Towers, which are even a little redder in color than the rest. All the walls and towers take their color from the ruddy soil; they are made of a combination of flint, earth and lime, called *chinarro*, which bakes in the sun to the hardness of stone.

These towers (1) stand apart from the enclosure of the Alhambra, upon a hill of their own, a little lower than the level of the adawes, from which people can be seen walking about upon the flat roofs which form a sort of terrace on top. This is the most ancient portion of Granada. It is mentioned by an Arabian poet of the middle century, as the Red Castle. Its long line of walls crown the hill and follow the curves and dips of the ground most gracefully.

After all, the wooded slopes of the approach to the Alhambra lend it one of its chiefest charms. They are kept green by the flowing channels of water, and kept alive by the song of many birds.

Wild as the spot may seem, it is yet the result of man's work, for it was the Moors who brought the streams, and changed the barren rock to this verdant retreat. The elm-trees were sent from England, 1812, to the governor of the Alhambra, as a present. They flourish well in the richly watered soil, although so unlike the trees which are native to it.

A couple of weeks slipped away like a flash in the enjoyment of this wonderful place, and Miss Lejeune and Bessie had not once descended so far as the Gate of the Entrance to the city of Granada. Mr. Horner had faithfully gone down at due intervals to visit the banker for letters, and he reported always on his return, strange sights he had seen, and hinted that these must not be neglected by the rest of the party. But Miss Augusta was too comfortable to lend an ear to this sort of talk. She was now leading precisely the life she enjoyed the most.

"What I like best in travelling," — she began one day to state —

"Is not to travel," suggested Mr. Horner, who was sitting

GLARING GRANADA.

fanning himself, and looking overwarm after a rapid walk through the glaring streets of the city. His hands were full of letters and newspapers, and he had just been saying to his assembled family, that they really must go with him the next time, and go through the Cathedral and other places.

— " is," resumed Miss Lejeune, scorning the interruption, "to be somewhere where there is enough to enjoy without going after it. Some people are chasing continually after the sights in a foreign town, and they are so tired after about a week of it that they do not know whether they are looking at a church or a Raphael."

GYPSY QUARTER.

"Do you think, aunt Dut, that even here we are quite near enough to the Alhambra?" asked Bessie. "Would it not be better if the Court of Lions was down below here under your window?"

"I think it would be better if we were actually in the enclosure; in a *Casa de Huespedes*. It would be lovely to stay there, and if I ever come again, that is what I shall do."

"When you and Mary come, you can have rooms in the house where the crazy man lives," said Tommy.

He referred to a mild, melancholy man whom they had met first wandering about the gypsy quarter; an American, who had accosted them when he heard them speaking English. He said he had been living there nearly a year, in a room which he hired not far from the palace, and within the walls. It was in a pretty little house at the end of a garden walk overhung with grapevine on an arched trellis, and his house-mates were a cat and a dog, and a friendly old señora, his landlady, who made him comfortable, and chatted with him in Spanish, which he knew from living many years in South America. Beyond this, his society was limited to chance acquaintances like the Horners, and they did not encourage him much, as subjects were few in common, and he was of a gloomy turn of mind.

When they had nothing better to talk about among themselves, they speculated upon his probable past, and imagined all sorts of reasons why he lived all by himself under the shadow of the tower of Comares.

"Perhaps he is digging for treasure," said Tommy.

"Perhaps he is a descendant of the Abencerrages," said Bessie.

He looked much more like a descendant of the Puritans, with a decidedly Yankee build and accent, in spite of a black beard, and a *sombrero* and *manta* such as the Spaniards wear.

Mr. Horner's private opinion was, that some slight misunderstanding with a parental government made it safer for him to avoid his native land, and to seek, perhaps, a place of some obscurity; but he did not think it worth while to express these views.

One day while they were having early coffee in the dining-room, the waiters told them with some excitement, that a man had been found dead that morning in the thicket below the Siete Suelos. A pistol-shot had been heard even at the distance of the hotel; and as a pistol was found lying near the body, it was supposed he had killed himself.

"It must be our crazy man!" exclaimed Bessie, "he was trying to get into the Treasure Vault of the Moors."

"Nonsense, Bessie!" said her father, rather sharply. "I must go and see about the matter."

As a fellow citizen, he felt it a point of duty to interest himself in the case.

On arriving at the spot where the victim of the accident was still lying, Mr. Horner was relieved to find that he did not recognize in him their man. He saw the body of a young Spaniard quite unknown to him. It was soon recognized by the authorities as that of a vagabond youth who for some time had been restlessly wandering about the grounds, and who had probably shot himself. But oddly enough, their American had disappeared. They never saw him again.

AT THE GATES OF A TOWN.
Paying Duty on Produce.

CHAPTER XXX.

THE CITY OF GRANADA.

MR. HORNER'S hints, and the necessity of the case, finally roused Miss Lejeune, and she consented to set about sight-seeing in good earnest. Their dreamy days in the Alhambra were at an end, and the rest of their time there was devoted to the Cathedral and the Convent of the Cartuja, and such points of interest as the city affords.

They thought the interior of the Cathedral very beautiful, although, perhaps because, entirely different from the Gothic grandeur of Burgos and Seville. There is nothing Gothic about it. It has Corinthian pillars, a dome, and noble rounded arches, with a profusion of white and gold decoration, which, strange to say, in Spain, never looks gaudy and tawdry, but solemn. The effect of gold in ornament is quiet instead of glaring, and as it is applied to the graceful curves of carving in the Spanish churches, it is at once rich and full of repose.

The chief ornaments of the Cimborio, under the dome, are seven grand pictures of the Virgin, painted by Alonzo Cano. They are very beautiful, although so high up that it is rather hard to see them, and of course impossible to examine them closely. Cano was the minor canon of this Cathedral, and he has enriched it with many works. He is buried there, under the choir.

Ferdinand and Isabella pervade the Cathedral, which was one of the chief glories of their reign. The Capilla de los Reyes, their royal chapel, is the most important part of it. It is adorned with the shields and badges of the Catholic sovereigns, as these two are always called. On each side of the high altar kneel effigies of the king and queen; exact representations of their faces, forms, and costumes; behind them are singular painted carvings of the work of their lives, the conquest of the Moors and the conversion of the infidels. In the one which illustrates the Alhambra, Isabella is riding

TOMB OF FERDINAND AND ISABELLA.

upon a white palfrey between Ferdinand and the great Cardinal Mendoza, who sits on a mule, holding out his hand for the key presented by Boabdil, dismounted. Behind are ladies, knights, and halberdiers, and captives are coming out of the gates.

Bessie looked a good while at this curious piece of carving; then she sighed deeply, and said:

"I knew we should have to hear all about Ferdinand and Isabella here, but I mean not to admire them any more than I can help."

In the centre of the chapel, the marble figures of the two sovereigns repose on alabaster sepulchres. The statue of Isabella is admirable. Her smile is cold and placid.

She died far from Granada, but desired to be buried in this Cathedral. In spite of her cruel policy to infidels, which naturally excited the displeasure of Bessie, Isabella was one of the best sovereigns who ever dignified a throne. Her time was the most brilliant period of Spanish history. The discovery of the New World, just when the Old World was found to be too narrow for the growth of human intellect and progress, was the great glory of her reign, although she herself doubtless thought the aid she promised to Columbus of trifling importance, compared with the surrender of that little key by the vanquished Moor.

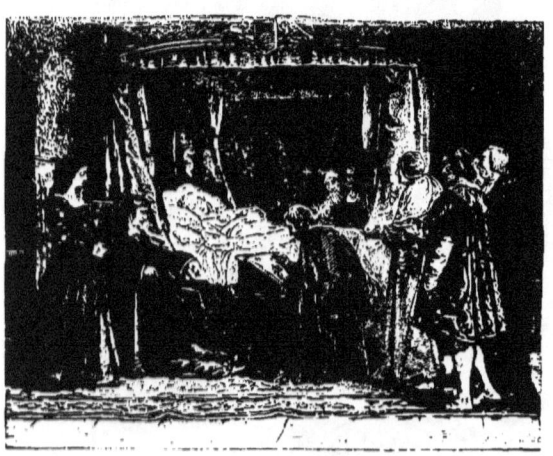

ELIZABETH DICTATING HER WILL.

The statue of Ferdinand is also lifelike. His head rests on the pillow without making an impression upon it, while that of the queen weighs it down. The Spaniards say it is because she had the most brains. But the king, her husband, was a wise, far-seeing monarch.

In the vault below, they are buried in plain coffins, which have never been disturbed. There also lies the body of their little grandson, Prince Miguel, who was thrown from his pony in a square in

Granada. If he had lived, he would have reigned over Spain and Portgual both, because his mother, the daughter of Ferdinand and Isabella, was married to the King of Portugal. The only son of the Catholic sovereigns died early; the throne passed to Tuana, who married Philip, son of the Emperor Maximilian. But this Philip died before Ferdinand did. It was his son Charles who became heir to the Spanish throne, and also later to the crown of the Emperor of Germany. Thus it was that the immense territories of the Netherlands, Germany, and Spain, were united under one monarch, Charles the Fifth.

Among the relics in the chapel, bequeathed to it by Ferdinand and Isabella, are the rare standards used at the conquest of Granada, and the sword of the king.

Near by hangs a portrait of the brave Ferdinand Perez de Pulgar, who performed a daring feat during the siege of Granada.

Indignant at an audacious act of one of the Moors, he went into the city one night with only a handful of followers, forced the gate, and galloped furiously through the streets to the principal mosque. Here he sprang from his horse, and, kneeling, took possession of the place, dedicating it to the Blessed Virgin as a Christian chapel. After nailing to the door with his dagger, a tablet inscribed with the words "*Ave Maria*," he remounted his horse and galloped back to the gate. The city was now aroused, but Ferdinand, overturning some and cutting down others, rejoined his companions outside the walls, and they all made good their way to the camp. This mosque became afterwards the Cathedral of Granada, and the Emperor, Charles the Fifth, conferred on the descendants of Pulgar the right of burial in that church, and the privilege of sitting in the choir during High Mass.

"I think," said Tommy, "that the Spaniards were just as noble as the Moors. I mean to leave off mourning for Boabdil!"

"Very well," replied Bessie. "I shall be faithful to the last."

This was almost the last they saw of the Moors, as they did not go to Valencia, where they would have found again traces of their industry and wealth, of a period earlier than that of the prosperity of Granada. Valencia became a Moorish kingdom, independent of the Cordovan Khalifate, in 1056; it was captured by the Cid at the end of the eleventh century, and never returned to the rule of the Moors. James the First of Aragon conquered it from the Cid, in the beginning of the thirteenth century, and later it was annexed to the crowns of Castile and Aragon.

The town of Granada proved not especially amusing. The Zacatin is the shopping street. It is occupied by little bazaars, with the usual gay panuelas and alforcas and mantas hanging out in the streets.

HOUSE IN GRANADA.

They visited the Cactuja, a suppressed convent outside the town. It was once enormously wealthy; founded by the Carthusian monks, on ground granted to them by the Gran Capitan, Gonsalvo de Cordova. The doors of the chapel are curiously inlaid with ebony, mother-of-pearl, and tortoise-shell, and there is a beautiful Virgin and Child, by Alonzo Cano. Miss Lejeune longed for photographs of this and of the masterpieces in the Cathedral, but they are not to be had. All these pictures are placed too high to be easily photographed, even if permission could be obtained for it; and in many cases, the chapels where fine pictures are hidden, in Spain, are so dark that photography would be impossible.

Gonsalvo de Cordova is almost as great a hero as the Cid himself. He was born in 1453, in a warlike and turbulent period, and at an early age attached himself to the fortunes of Isabella. At her court, his beauty and knightly deeds soon attracted attention; in the long war of Granada, his military discipline was perfected,

PALMS AT ELCHE.

though he was then too young to occupy the most eminent position. After the war he became a brilliant ornament of the royal circle. His manners wore the gallantry of the time, as is shown by the anecdote of the queen's wardrobe at Sante Fe. He was sent by King Ferdinand to Sicily in 1495, to resist the pretensions of

Charles the Eighth of France to the throne of Naples; and there Gonsalvo showed great bravery and daring, although forced to retreat after one battle; the only one which he lost during his long and fortunate career. In less than a year he made himself master of the larger part of the kingdom of Naples. It was then that he received by general consent the title of the Great Captain.

The total expulsion of the French was the result of his victories, and the submission of the last rood of territory possessed by Charles the Eighth in the Kingdom of Naples.

Gonsalvo continued in Naples, ruling the kingdom as viceroy, until Ferdinand recalled him, apparently suspecting that he meant to make himself an independent sovereign.

He was received at home with the highest distinction, and lived from this time upon his own estates in great magnificence. The king treated him with coldness, jealous, perhaps, of his popularity; but after his death, the king and court went into mourning, and the whole of Spain lamented his loss.

As they did not go to Valencia, they missed Elche, where are some fine palms, in almost the only grove of them in Spain. They would have enjoyed this excursion, but, as Bessie said:

"We had palms in the East."

CHAPTER XXXI.

BESSIE TO MARY.

THURSDAY was occupied in last things. The end of the afternoon was spent once more in the garden of the Torre de la Vela. Aunt Dut was finishing her sketch of the Sierra Nevada, all rosy and snow-capped, with great red geraniums close to us for the foreground. The people of the garden were very friendly, like all such people in Spain; far from being bandits, they are always standing around with watering-pots; sometimes old gentlemen, sometimes very pretty señoras, who put roses in papa's button-hole. To be sure they all like a peseta at parting, but who does not?

"Our trunks had to be packed that evening, for on Friday morning (at half-past three, my dear; how would you have liked that?) we were dragged

POSTILION.

from our beds, in order to be down in Granada to take the diligence at five. The berlina of this diligence answers to the coupé that you are accustomed to, the *cupé* of Spain being a less distinguished place on top. We had engaged the berlina, but it only held three; so that papa and

Tommy took turns in climbing up to a seat by the driver, a splendid place where they could see all the country, though they had nothing much to their backs, and papa's legs hung down so that we had a sight of his heels to comfort us. The door of our place was very small; I doubt if Mrs. Stuyvesant could have squeezed herself into it. We sat within our little glass-case, all among the legs of the horses, and packed so solid with our hand-bags and straps, alpacas and lunch-bags, that we could not stir. There was a sort of shelf just outside our windows, where a stout Spaniard came and sat most of the time, so that the view in front was very

ON THE VEGA.

much filled up. Nevertheless, we had a jovial day, reaching Jaen at half-past one P. M. The horses, chiefly mules, were eight; two abreast. On the forward off mule sat a postilion, jouncing up and down in the saddle, but occasionally springing off to run all around the whole team, and larrup the beasts, who then ran at their utmost, raising great clouds of white dust. The coach swayed, the mayoral yelled, there was a tremendous uproar, as if it were a change of government, in spite of which this youth would turn up from behind, overtake his forward steed, and jump into the saddle again. The result of these uprisings was brief; all the mules settled down again into a jog directly, and then the postilion came and reposed a few moments on the bench in front of us, and smoked a cigarette until he felt a call to renew the scene. The animals were changed often at little villages, and then papa came and chatted, and changed places with Tommy. There was not much room for papa inside with us. His hat scraped the ceiling, and the front wall of our abode scraped his knees.

"Meanwhile the scenery was wonderful. After we had crossed the Vega with its *huertas* scattered along, the road wound about in zigzags like a Swiss pass. The mountains took on beautiful pink tints with blue shadows, and always such flowers! poppies, bluets, — things we knew, things we did not know. I saw a little boy sitting under an olive-tree, beside a basket full of apricots, with his face smeared from ear to ear with mulberry-juice. Once, when we stopped, I gathered a spray of white clematis, just like ours at home, growing on a pomegranate-tree all in blossom.

"It grew pretty hot and glaring as we came up the hill to Jaën, and we were covered with thick, powdery white dust, especially myself; for when I crawled out of our little door to get the clematis, I knocked my hat off, and it fell, top downward, into a bed of dust, which penetrated it, so that it is no longer a dark-blue felt. By the way, we have had such a time about straw hats; you know we thought we could buy them anywhere as soon as the warm weather demanded them. On the contrary, the Spanish do not wear hats. Their heads are tied up in panuelas, most picturesque, but not shady. It was not till we reached Malaga that we could find any straw hats. There we bought one apiece, all alike, for a peseta each. At Granada, I trimmed them all with white scarfs, — papa's and Tommy's, as well as ours. They accompany us in a strap with the lunch-box, and were part of the furniture of our berlina." . . .

Jaën is the capital of the province of the same name. The Horners had left Andalusia behind. They saw no more Moorish balconies; no more cacti and aloes. These had given place to more Northern products of the soil. The diligence road on which they had come, brought them to a point very near Menjibar, a station on the same railway over which they had passed when

SPANISH BALCONIES.

they went from Madrid to Cordova and the South. They were thus about to take up the line of their travels, and retrace their steps to Madrid.

They did not stop at Jaën, though it is an interesting old

town. There was time to step across the plaza and look at the cathedral, a fine building of the sixteenth century, noble within though much defaced by whitewash.

They had an excellent almuerzo at an unpretending little fonda, for which they were quite ready, after their early coffee at half-past three. To be sure the lunch-basket had been consulted in the interval, and bits of chicken had disappeared.

PARTING AT THE STATION.

An omnibus rattled them to the railway-station, where of course, there was an hour or more to wait. Tommy fed the chickens belonging to the señora, who kept a "cooling-drinks" stand outside.

An immense crowd collected and departed while they were waiting, for another train carried off a number of recruits for the army, and the whole population turned out to see them off, although they were going to no dangerous exposure in this wonderfully peaceful period for Spain.

Miss Lejeune looked about for something to sketch, but the region was as barren as a junction always is in New England, and wore the same brand-new, incomplete aspect. Spanish railways are too modern to share the picturesque qualities of their country.

Now came another long journey in the train,— the most fatiguing of the Horners' experience. It was hot and glaring all day; the scenery was uninteresting, and the long hours of the hot day were followed by a night of the same stiff positions, tumbled hair and unwashed faces.

In the middle of the night, they passed through the place where they had bought the daggers. All roused themselves this time to go after chocolate. The scene repeated itself. The vender of knives appeared, and they bought more, proud this time of the improvement in their Spanish, which enabled them to hold a parley with the dagger-merchant. But this was but a break in the misery of the night. Glad they were to see the dawn, after doubtful slumbers; and still more glad to find themselves in the great station at Madrid, which now seemed like home.

Home it might be, but repose was not yet for their weary limbs. Miss Lejeune had written for an apartment in a *casa de huespedes*, of which she had the address, and having received a favorable answer, had taken the rooms conditionally. Their omnibus now drove them to this house in Calle Mayor, 21, an excellent position, just off the gay Puerta del Sol. While the children remained with the vehicle, Mr. Horner and Miss Augusta climbed the stairs with a very obliging landlord, to look at the rooms and see if they would answer.

Tommy was on the sidewalk staring about him like one in a dream suddenly set down in a strange place which seems strangely familiar. Suddenly he heard a shout above him, and looking up, he saw in a little balcony in the third story, his father and Miss Lejeune, waving and both beckoning.

SPANISH DILIGENCE.

Bessie came quickly out of the omnibus, her hair in a sadly rumpled condition, and the once dark-blue hat, now powdered with white, lamentably jammed on one side. They seized bags and bundles. The blue-bloused conductor of the carriage armed himself also, and soon they were climbing up the narrow stairs to their new abode. A door, with a bell-pull, on the third landing, stood open. Miss Lejeune awaited them in the entrance. They passed through a little dining-room, with a window upon a little court, or wall, and found themselves in a long, pleasant salon, rather meagrely furnished, but with the usual allowance of clocks and mirrors which France has bequeathed to all European hotels.

"Is it not cosey?" demanded Miss Lejeune.

"Do you think it will do?" asked the father, a little anxious.

"I think it is delicious!" said Bessie, casting a rapid glance about, "only I have not seen it at all yet."

"Well, then we will decide to stay," said Mr. Horner, with a sigh of relief. Miss Lejeune nodded with a pleasant smile to the landlord and his wife, and thus their life in a Spanish boarding-house began.

Señor Rico and his friendly spouse could speak no word of any language but Spanish; no more could the active maid Rita, who did the work; far less the long-limbed, gaunt, elderly char-woman who appeared and disappeared very mysteriously from the kitchen department, which was just across the little brick-tiled passage-way. The Horners gloried in their daring which allowed them to attempt living in this way.

It worked perfectly well, and proved much pleasanter than hotel-life, at any rate, for a change, while it was, of course, cheaper. The rooms all opened from each other, and it was necessary to go through Mr. Horner's bedroom to reach the salon; but this did not signify, as they did not expect visits from the grandees of Spain. The salon and Miss Augusta's room overlooked the street and the square, with large windows *à double battants*, and little balconies. The rooms were high enough from the street to avoid the worst of the noise, and Miss Lejeune enjoyed being awakened every morning in the early dawn by the tender bray of the donkeys who drag the little milk-carts and barrows of vegetables which aged señoras sell about the streets.

Later, the music of large, well-built hand-organs floated up to them, playing charming Aragoneses, Jotas, Jaleos, with something of the same *verve* they received from the light-hearted, light-fingered artists strumming the guitar before the Siete Suelos, at the Alhambra.

CHAPTER XXXII.

THE PICTURE GALLERY.

MADRID has the reputation of a bad climate, extremely cold in winter, and hot in summer. The Horners had been warned not to stay there too late, on account of the danger to health from the difference of temperature between sun and shade in the summer months, and especially the difference between the cold of the galleries and the warm outside air.

But they had lovely weather all the time. It was the middle of June, and neither too hot nor too cold; and they reached the conclusion that the climate had been calumniated.

The chief inducement to a long stay in Madrid is the gallery of pictures called the Museo Reale, which Miss Lejeune especially wished to study thoroughly. She sat down before it as one who would besiege a city, and made it her regular morning occupation to go to the Prado after coffee and stay till almuerzo at twelve. The rest showed the same zeal for a day or two, but although they fell off sooner or later, she had not the slightest objection to be there alone. The permission to draw there is easily obtained through the kindness and liberality of the director of the Museum, and though Miss Lejeune set up no large easel to attack a Velasquez or a Ribera, as she saw many a brave young artist doing with good success, she transferred to her sketch book souvenirs and snatches of parts of her favorite pictures, and made notes of their coloring, to help Mary to understand the photographs which she bought for her before leaving Madrid, from Laurent's excellent collection. Mr. Horner found, as he expected, a budget of letters and papers from his partners, on a special question of business, and he settled himself every morning at the writing table in their salon, to study them and to write full instructions to those at home. After Bessie had written and despatched one epistle of many sheets to her mother, reviewing all the Alhambra experiences, which she had had little time to write about while they were there, she was ready for expeditions, and with Tommy, started off whenever he felt inclined. She could "do" enough Spanish to make her way anywhere. Tom, on the contrary, never acquired the language beyond ordering *horchata de chufas* in a café.

INTERIOR OF THE ARMORY.

Thus these two saw more of the streets, churches, and shops than their elders. The afternoons were devoted by all to excursions in various directions, the favorite of which was the drive in the Buen Retiro gardens.

They went one day to the Armory, because Bessie wished to see the sword of Pelayo, mentioned in the list in the guide-book. As there was likely to be some difficulty about admission, Rico, the friendly and alert landlord, went with them on this occasion. The Armory is a part of the royal palace, and at first they were refused admittance by the guard at the door. After a parley with Rico, he said they might perhaps obtain permission by applying to the director, who was to be seen in the Palace. After crossing the large courtyard and corridors, they were admitted to a waiting-room in the Palace, where gold-buttoned valets with red waistcoats, were gliding in and out. They had armed themselves with their passports, for which, by the way, they now found a use for the first and last time in Spain; and after these had been duly examined, a highly distinguished old gentleman, with perhaps the blue blood of Pelayo in his veins, courteously gave them permission to visit the Armory, and sent a special person in buttons, to escort them back across the hot, glaring courtyard.

When they found themselves fairly within the Armory, it proved that it was undergoing what we should call a spring cleaning, and was, in consequence, all up in arms. This did not, however, prevent them from seeing all the curiosities, and it was highly entertaining to watch a group of dressmakers putting clothes upon wooden figures which were to display the armor and costume of ancient periods. It is a remarkable collection, well worth seeing. Charles the Fifth, and Philip the Second, in full armor, sit upon their splendidly caparisoned war-horses, as they are represented in the portraits by Titian, and other heroes display, in effigy, the corselets, shields and weapons of their time.

There are longer expeditions from Madrid to places of interest. One of these is to the gridiron-shaped Escurial, built by Philip the Second as a mausoleum for the royal family of Spain. The Horners, to tell the truth, regarded this excursion with fear and trembling, and Miss Lejeune refused from the first, to have anything to do with it. "The idea of the Escurial," she said, "is dismal enough, and I have no wish to visit it." She held to her opinion, even when they returned full of enthusiasm for the grand, though gloomy edifice, where, in an oratory, are kneeling effigies of Charles the Fifth, and Philip the Second, with their wives and daughters; all portraits executed with skill.

The library is a long and beautiful room, intended by Philip the Second to be on the same scale of magnificence as the rest of the Escurial. The collection of books was once one of the

THE GRIDIRON-SHAPED ESCURIAL.

richest in Europe, but it is now much diminished through neglect, the invasion of the French, and other theft.

Another longer expedition was to Aranjuez, and this was shared by Miss Lejeune. They spent the day wandering about the charming gardens, under the tall elms brought from England by Philip the Second, listening to nightingales and cuckoos. They spent the night at a small inn upon a wide, dusty street. Just as they entered it, a violent thunder storm began, which crashed and rolled all night, while the rain poured down. It was all over before the morning, fortunately, and they returned to Madrid in bright sunshine, not without turning their eyes with longing back toward

Toledo, which is upon the same railroad, but farther away from Madrid.

"Dear Toledo!" said Bessie; "how long it seems since we were there. I wonder how the señoras are getting along!"

LIBRARY OF THE ESCURIAL.

"I wish they could hear our improved Spanish," said Miss Lejeune.

"I had Hubert then," remarked Tommy gloomily.

The boys had kept up an active correspondence since the parting. Although letter-writing was an immense effort to the youngest Horner, he wished to impart all his observations to the companion who had shared the first part of the Spanish experience; and this overcame his aversion to putting pen to paper.

Hubert's letters in return were better written and better spelled, but shorter, for he had nothing to communicate which Tom could take an interest in. His chief subject was comment on the wonders in Tom's letters, and a constant undertone of longing to be back with the family who had been so kind to him.

Aranjuez was a favorite resort of the Catholic sovereigns, and since then has been occupied and improved by almost every king. Philip the Fifth, the Bourbon, caused a new set of buildings to be erected in the Louis the Fourteenth style, and the effect is that of a Spanish Fontainebleau. The court still resides here every year for a few weeks.

Ferdinand and Isabella were true Spanish sovereigns. By their marriage, the different provinces of the Peninsula were united, and a purely national period ensued. But their son did not live to reign, and by the marriage of their daughter Juana, to a prince of Austria, Philip, the son of the Emperor Maximilian, a foreign element was introduced, which was to unite the empire of Germany with the kingdom of Spain. Thus Charles the First, of Spain, is better known by his title of Charles the Fifth, Emperor of Germany, and he and his direct descendants, who occupied the throne of Spain for more than a century, are called the sovereigns of the Austrian house.

The dominions of Charles the Fifth extended over half of Europe. He inherited, through his father, the portion of Burgundy which contained the Netherlands. He was elected to the imperial crown of Germany, and his domain was further enlarged by the empires of the New World, which the discovery of Columbus gave to Spain. Thus Spain filled a minor place in his great territory, and while the rest of Europe became the theatre of the great battle for religious liberty, roused by the appearance of Martin

Luther, her people were allowed to cultivate the arts of peace. At last Charles the Fifth, tired of governing so large a realm, retired to the convent of Yuste, and left the throne to his son, Philip the Second. This prince was born and educated in Spain, and imbibed, or inherited, all the peculiarities of the national character. He was gloomy, stern, and bigoted, yet in general, swayed by a strict sense of justice. With him ends the greatness of the kingdom; for during the reign of his successors, Spain lost the glory

THE ENGLISH ELMS, ARANJUEZ.

she had attained. Philip the Third expelled all the remaining Moors, and thus deprived the country of their industry and wealth. Philip the Fourth lost many of the possessions of the kingdom, which became, in his time, reduced almost to the limits of the Peninsula.

Charles the Second, the son of Philip the Fourth, inherited the throne. He died without children, in 1698, and now began the celebrated war of the Spanish Succession, in which all Europe joined, which forms a part of English history, including the triumphs of Marlborough, as well as a long page in the annals of France. It ended in the accession of a Bourbon to the Spanish throne,— Philip, Duke of Anjou, grandson of Louis the Fourteenth, who thus became Philip the Fifth. He was not a very different Philip from those who preceded him, although born and bred at the French Court.

With many reverses, the Bourbons have held the Spanish throne since his accession in 1700.

Napoleon interfered with their rights in the early part of this century, and since then there have been many attempts at republican government, and periods of great confusion and anarchy. At the present time, a liberal monarchy seems secure in the hands of the young king Alphonso, who occupies the throne, a descendant of Philip the Fifth, the Bourbon.

CHAPTER XXXIII.

SPANISH ART.

PHILIP THE SECOND, like his father, Charles the Fifth, was devoted to art, and through their influence, their country is a treasury of wonderful interest. Titian was the painter that Charles the Fifth delighted most to honor, and his son Philip shared this ardor; to their patronage the world is indebted for some of this great master's noblest productions. Philip built the Escurial, and sent to Italy, where art was then in its glory, for artists to decorate its walls and ceilings; and at his court artists were treated with the highest consideration, — on the same footing with haughty grandees of Spain.

The characteristic of Spanish art is its religious tendency. It was cultivated in its early period, not for its own sake, but as illustrating religious subjects, for the adornment of cathedrals, and to elevate the human mind by contemplation of divine images.

The pictures of the early Spanish masters, therefore, are full of religious sentiment, and great beauty of feeling; the principal period is in the sixteenth and seventeenth centuries, encouraged by the high favor of the court. Under the Bourbon princes, the French school has prevailed, and the Spanish artists have departed from their national characteristics; but of late, Fortuny, Madrazo, and others, have produced something like a modern Spanish school, with a charm of its own.

The pictures of Spain, which were scattered throughout the cathedrals and churches, were many of them carried off by the French, under Napoleon's directions, after the manner of that conqueror; and there are still to be seen at the Louvre, and elsewhere outside of their native country, fine specimens of Spanish art. But the greater part of these treasures are now collected in the Royal Museum at Madrid. It is said that Joseph Bonaparte, during his brief sojourn in the capital, suggested and decreed the formation of a National Gallery of paintings; but it was not until 1819 that the present building was devoted to the purpose. Ferdinand the Seventh caused it to be thrown open to the public, with about three hundred Spanish pictures. Since then many more have been added from the Escurial and other royal palaces; originals of undoubted authenticity, because they were taken directly from the places for which they were painted. They now number upwards of two thousand, and are the property of the crown. The gallery is generally considered the finest in the world. It is a collection of splendid gems, rather than a chronological series of pictures of different schools, like that at Berlin, which is wonderfully complete in that regard.

Here Miss Lejeune delighted to wander in the long cool galleries, catalogue in hand; and here Bessie often joined her, for apart from the artistic interest of the pictures, there was a great one for such a student of history as Bessie. The walls are plentifully hung with portraits of historic value painted by the celebrated artists of their time. Titian's Charles the Fifth on horseback gives a vivid revelation of the stern conqueror, with heavy Austrian jaw and determined brow. His wife, the Empress, Doña Isabel, of Portugal, also by Titian, and Philip the Second, are there too, to help the impression of their characters, acquired in reading of their deeds. Bessie liked them far better than the Venus and Adonises, the Dianas and Acteons of Titian, which she pronounced to be too much like the Virgins and Magdalens of the same painter. Two charming pictures of Carlos, the son of Philip the Second, and his sister Isabella Clara, by Sanchez Coello, were favorites not only with Bessie, but all the rest. Pantoja de la Cruz, a pupil of Coello, painted also portraits of Empresses and Infantas, bristling with the stiffness and formality of the court costume of his time, the sixteenth century, their throats buried in high stiff ruffs, and each looking, as Tommy considered, as if she had swallowed a poker.

THE DWARF "EL PRIMO" — *Velasquez.*

The great master of the time of Philip the Fourth, Velasquez, claimed the most of their attention. Nowhere but in this gallery can his paintings be seen to advantage. A large portion of the walls along the room are occupied with his works, some of them very large, representing scenes, historical or allegorical, crowded with figures, nobly executed. In the same room hang the many Murillos belonging to this gallery, but Seville has not surrendered those in her possession; and there the Horners had already gained their impression of his graceful, tender Madonnas, and delicate coloring. Mr. Horner was extremely fond of them and glad to have a chance to see more.

Besides the Spanish school, there are rooms full of other masterpieces; the ground floor of the palace, below the principal gallery, contains an extremely interesting collection of early Flemish and German works. Here it was that Miss Lejeune sighed for

VELASQUEZ.

Mary's sympathetic presence. "Where is Augusta?" asked Mr. Horner one day when he joined Bessie, by appointment, in the Oval Room, or Sala Isabel the Second.

"She is down among her Early Flemish," replied Bessie. "She has discovered a Patinir of rare merit, and I believe she means to copy it for Mary."

"A what?" demanded her father.

"A Patinir. He was a man, papa, that painted pictures. I will go and find aunt Dut."

"No; only tell me where to go, and I will find her."

He discovered her committing the Patinir to memory, to be able to paint it afterwards. It was very Early Flemish, and represented the Flight into Egypt. Mr. Horner thought it a confused mass of badly done figures in impossible positions, but Miss Lejeune convinced him that the landscape which formed the background was lovely.

The Sala Isabel the Second is an oval gallery, with a railing, open to the hall underneath it, which is thus lighted from the dome above. The walls are hung with the gems of the whole collection; Raphael, Rubens, and Vandyck are well represented. In this room is the portrait of Queen Mary of England, — Bloody Mary, who was the wife of Philip the Second. This was painted by Antonio Moro, as he is called in Spain, a native of Utrecht, called in Dutch catalogues Antony Mor. The long connection of Spain with the Netherlands gave to the nation so great a number of Flemish pictures.

FROM EQUESTRIAN PORTRAIT OF PHILIP IV. — *Velasquez.*

"Come away; come away!" exclaimed Mr. Horner; "you have had enough for one day, and besides, you will be here again tomorrow. It is lovely out-doors. I have a carriage below, and

Tommy is waiting in it, with piles of letters from the bankers."

This was enough. Miss Augusta turned away at once from the Rembrandt she was examining, and they hastened through the long rooms, unobservant this time of the Titians that looked down upon them from the walls.

A gentleman they called the Amateur, because he was always in the gallery, to fill up his time, apparently, listlessly looking at the pictures, but with more animation at the visitors, raised his hat as they passed.

It was bright and sunny, and the air felt soft after the chilly atmosphere of the gallery. They were soon driving along the Prado, in a wide, open carriage, so busy with their letters that they noticed nothing

PAUL REMBRANDT

around them. An exclamation of more than usual vigor, from Mr. Horner, made them put down the sheets they were reading. All listened, while he exclaimed: —

"Philip has a plan! I see no objection to it yet. This is what he says:" —

DEAR PAPA: I hope you will write me at once, and very distinctly, what you mean to do on leaving Madrid. Ever since we heard you were thinking of Saragossa, I have been possessed of an idea to which mamma does not object, and if you approve, I think it will be very easy to carry it out. We are very near the Spanish frontier here, and I know that I can perfectly well cross the mountains on horseback, and come down and meet you at Saragossa —

"Meet us!" exclaimed all, with one accord.

There is a railroad (continued Mr. Horner, reading from the letter) from Saragossa to a place called Huesca, and between that and the frontier an excellent diligence road. I can find out more about my connections, if I hear from you that you consent to the plan. As for mamma and Mary, they think they can manage to do without me —

The letter went on to explain how easy it would be for the two ladies to come alone to join the rest of the party at Marseilles.

THE AMATEUR.

Mrs. Horner wrote herself to advocate the plan.

"Give me the guide-book!" said Miss Lejeune. "I have seen that road on the map."

O'Shea's guide was always with them, on the cushion of the carriage, or under somebody's arm. It had been lost a dozen times, and its binding, once fresh, had assumed a weather-beaten air, but it had a wonderful faculty for being found, and for turning up just at the right moment; and this is a great merit in a guide-book.

"See!" said Miss Lejeune, opening the book at one of the maps. "Here they are at Luz; he can get somehow over the mountains to Panticosa, or this little place Jaca, and then come down to Huesca, where the rail begins."

Whether he would come to Panticosa or Jaca, and how he would get across the mountains, formed a subject of much discussion. The Horners asked Rico, and everybody else they knew in Madrid. Everybody was sure the thing could be done, but no one knew how. The maps and plans in their guide-books gave out at the Spanish boundary, and they had no Guide-Joanne to consult.

SPANISH ART.

"But they have," said Bessie, "and they have studied up by this time. The thing is, papa, to tell Philip he may come!"

"And at what hotel to meet us!" added Miss Lejeune.

"And the name of the banker, if we can find that out."

"O papa! they have the same letter of credit."

"True enough," replied her father; "but," he continued, beginning to worry a little, after the manner of parents, "I do not feel sure that he will be able to make his way without knowing Spanish."

CHAPTER XXXIV.

KING ALPHONSO.

DRIVING up the Calle Jeronimo, Miss Lejeune said:
"As we are so near home, do you mind stopping for a moment for my parasol? This sun is really penetrating to-day."

The order was given, and Tommy begged to be allowed to run up the four flights which led to their second floor.

It was a fortunate chance which led them to pause at their house, for Rico came out to meet them at the carriage, with some cards in his hand, which had just been left by the American minister, admitting them to a *conferencia* of the "Association de Agricultores de España," in the Botanical Garden, at which the king would probably be present.

"The king!" cried Bessie; "when is it?"

"At this moment, señora," replied Rico. "I have been watching anxiously for your return. If your worships will drive there at once, you will, I think, not be too late."

Tommy appeared with the parasol, breathless.

"Jump, in Tommy!" cried his father. "Rico, tell the driver whatever means as fast as possible; if," he added in a lower tone, "there is any word in Spanish that means. the reverse of slow."

Rico's word to the coachman, whatever it was, had good effect, for they soon found themselves at the entrance of the garden, and, following the crowd, reached a portion of it protected from the sun by awnings, and decorated with Spanish flags. A sort of baldachino, under which dignitaries were to be seated, was prettily festooned with the national colors, red and yellow. Well dressed ladies, for the most part, occupied the garden chairs, placed in rows before this tent, and chatted with each other in low tones. A fair pro-

PRINCE BALTHAZAR CHARLES, SON OF PHILIP THE FOURTH. —*Velasquez.*

TO VIKU
IN PROFILIA

portion of gentlemen, with bald heads, and tiny orders at the button-hole, were sprinkled in the group. The sky was very blue overhead, and where the sun poured through the openings of the leaves, on the awning, gay parasols were necessary.

After awhile a slight commotion announced the approach of the royal party. Every one stood up, the gentlemen took off their hats, all eyes were turned towards the group.

It was not like seeing Boabdil (wrote Bessie) nor yet like Ferdinand and Isabella; and it was quite painful to see how little crown he had on, being clothed, in fact, like any young man of five and twenty; but thus it is with kings nowadays!

The young man walked quickly up the passage, bowing courteously with a pleasant smile on his face, to those who greeted him. He was followed by his ministers, all sage-looking, older men. They seated themselves under the draped awning, and listened gravely to a discourse upon "*Los aliados del labrador en su lucha entomologica,*" which, if it was tedious to the Horners, who did not make out a quarter of it, must have been still more so to those who under-

ENTRANCE TO BOTANICAL GARDEN.

stood the whole. It was soon over, however, and after a few brief words from the king, of thanks to the speaker of the day, the conference broke up. The Horners had the luck to reach the great gateway just as his Majesty was climbing into a light dogcart. He took the reins himself, the groom sprang up behind him, and he drove off, bowing to right and left.

Our republicans gazed at the spectacle of royal simplicity, with a shade of depression. Tommy grumbled :

"He might just as well be a member of Congress."

"How glad he must be to escape from the grand coach of state," said Bessie.

"I wonder which horse that is!"

Rico had taken the children one day to see the royal stables, which contain upwards of three hundred horses, and two hundred mules; long-maned horses of the cream color, called Isabelle, from

STATE CARRIAGES.

the color of the lace Queen Isabella wore. It was she who set the fashion of never washing her laces, according to Spanish report. The mules are first-rate, and much admired by connoisseurs. In the early Spanish wars, it was found that mules were used so much instead of horses, that a law was made, forbidding all warriors to ride them, and limiting them to churchmen and monks. Since then many a cardinal has been proud to possess mules of great beauty and strength for his state equipage.

The coach-houses contain all sorts of vehicles, some of them presents from sovereigns, of great splendor, and also, it must be said, of great clumsiness.

Madrid has not always been the capital of Spain. It had no great importance until, in the sixteenth century, it became the constant residence of Charles the Fifth. The climate was well suited to the nerves of the Emperor, who feared the earthquakes of Granada, and cared not to stay at Toledo, which was the capital, while Madrid was but a hunting-box. Philip, carrying out the idea of his father, declared Madrid the only court of the kingdom, being himself resolved to live mostly at the Escurial, which is not far off. It was, on the whole, a wise measure, as it centralized the power in a new city free from the local prejudices of separate provinces. Philip did not live to carry out all the plans he had formed for his new capital. His successor, Philip the Third, held his court at Valladolid, but the climate of that city is not suited for a capital. The Bourbon Philip the Fifth, and Charles the Third, added much to the beauty of Madrid, and it is now certainly a brilliant, clean, well-paved and well-lighted city.

The Horners loved it. No other foreign city, — and they had passed the same length of time on many, — gave them the same

ROYAL STABLES.

sense of homelike, cheerful friendliness. The people in the streets were always kindly and gay. Politeness is a custom, not a matter of choice. Even the lazy fellow who sells cooling drinks at the street corner, touches his cap, and offers conscientious change for the smallest of coins. There is much life and movement in the streets, and though, as is constantly said, the national costume is disappearing, some picturesque figures are yet to be seen here and there. The mantilla and manta have not given place altogether to the French bonnet and tight-fitting coat. In fact, the Horners, in

Spain, became so familiar with short breeches, and buttons up the leg, of all good Spaniards, that it was almost a shock to them to see the draggling trousers hanging about the feet of the inhabitants of the rest of Europe.

The Calle de Toledo is the most Spanish-looking street in the capital. It is crooked, and on a downward slope. The houses are

COOLING DRINKS.

old, and booths stand on the sidewalk, hung with gay and cheap pannelas, worsted stockings, and toys for children. El Rastro is a kind of pawnshop, or auction-room, where all sorts of wonders are bid off for a trifle. Here the knowing ones pick up pieces of tapestry, rare old Spanish embroidery, and bits of real church-lace, for a song; but it is an ordeal involving smells and dirt, and great danger of being cheated, for there is no quarter of the world where second-hand antiquities are exchanged *sans peur et sans reproche*.

It was here that Tommy got lost one day. He missed an appointment with Bessie and Rico, by waiting too long at the bank with his father. When he reached home alone, he found the apartment deserted, and a brief note stuck high up on top of the lamp-chimney, to attract his attention, saying:

Waited till quarter of eleven. Suppose you do not care to go. BESSIE.

Master Tom, finding himself thrown upon his own resources, thought he would take a turn alone through the streets, and after studying the plan of Madrid in the guide-book, he set forth in search of adventures, determined to strike for unknown parts of the town. He knew his way across the Puerta del Sol, and down to the Prado, as well as the main street in Keene, N. H., and he thought it would be fine to make new discoveries. So he turned into the Plaza Mayor, and walked along under the arcade, looking into shop

OLD SPANISH EMBROIDERY.

windows, and then without difficulty found himself going down Toledo street in the right direction. The booths amused him. He bought a tinsel pin-case of an ancient señora with but one tooth. Finding he had come out without a pocket-handkerchief, he bought a very gaudy one for eight cents, with a yellow border, stamped with blue crosses. It was not hemmed, and proved to be of pure cotton; but it answered his immediate purpose. He came to a sort of meat-market of odds and ends for sale, such as are not familiar to American children; terrible things without a name, in Tommy's experience.

Passing hastily through this row of booths, he perceived that the street was full of evil-looking people, quite different from the elegant loungers of the Puerta del Sol. They were gypsies, perhaps, or Jews; at any rate, lawless-looking people. They stared at him, and occasionally said things to him which, of course, he did not understand. He began to wish he had not come, and hastily turned into a quieter-looking street, which ought to bring him out on one of those he knew. He walked and walked through deserted thoroughfares, without shops and with stately houses, all lonely. No carts or foot-passengers were passing. Wherever a turning allowed, he went downhill, hoping to reach one of the Rondas, a succession of streets or boulevards which surround the town. He did, at last, and found himself on a wide, dusty, unpaved road, with high walls on the side of the city, and on the other a broad, desolate stretch not unlike Shanty-town, outside the park at New York. It was hot. The noon sun poured down upon him. It seemed an endless time before he reached the familiar Calle de Atocha, and saw at the same time the fountains of the Prado.

There was still a long walk up the steep hill to the Puerta del Sol; after that, a few steps brought him to their house.

Rico stood in the doorway, tearing his hair (figuratively). Almuerzo had long been over, and the family were in alarm. Master Tom was very hot, very hungry, and a little bit cross.

GATE OF HOSPICIO.

TOREROS ENTERING THE ARENA.

CHAPTER XXXV.

PERRO PACO.

EVEN American women whom the Horners met in Spain said they really must see a bull-fight, although one of them herself admitted that she had fainted when a horse was killed, and had to be carried out of the building. But they firmly resisted; in fact, firmness was not required, for no one wished to go. Mr. Horner did not choose to countenance any performance of which his moral nature so wholly disapproved.

Miss Lejeune could not bear the thought of going for an instant. Bessie belonged to the Society for the Prevention of Cruelty to Animals, and the fear of

Mr. Bergh, and her love for a kind friend at home, devoted to that cause, would have kept her away even if curiosity and inclination had drawn her towards the spectacle. Tommy may have had a secret feeling that "the other boys" he knew would expect him to have been to a bull-fight; in fact, he consulted his father privately, as to whether it might not be a good thing for him to go by himself, and see what it was.

"Do you really want to go?" asked his father.

"No!" replied Tommy, most sincerely, "but I thought perhaps it might seem — a little more manly to see the thing."

"Go, if you like, my son. Rico will go with you with joy; but, for my part, I think it is more manly to stay away."

Tommy said no more, and the last Sunday came and passed without his seeing a bull-fight.*

Sunday is the day for *corridas de Toros*, and during the season, no week passes without one in Madrid and Seville, while they occur often in other places.

The arena is a circular building, like the coliseum, with seats rising high above each other. It is open to the air above, the seats on the shady side commanding the highest price.

The entertainment is highly fashionable, and the chief argument for foreigners is, going to see the crowds of gayly dressed and animated spectators.

Spanish ladies are present, handsomely dressed as if for a ball, and the king usually honors the occasion. There are, however, many other opportunities for seeing royalty, and chances to inspect the beauty and fashion of the capital, even if less brilliant, are not accompanied by the painful spectacle of suffering creatures and human beings in danger.

There was one hero of the bull-ring whom they would all have liked to see, watching the performance, as he never failed to do.

This was PERRO PACO, an individual who just at the time the Horners were in Madrid, occupied the attention, and held the affections, of the whole population.

* Although the Horners did not see a bull-fight, some illustrations of the spectacle are inserted to show the cruel and bloody nature of the sport.

Perro Paco, as his name shows, was a dog, a real live dog, who lived at a restaurant in the Calle Alcala. Tommy saw him there one day, when he was pointed out to him by Rico; but as Tommy did not understand the Spanish description of him, he

TOREROS BEFORE THE CAFE DE PARIS.

failed to give him the amount of attention his reputation deserves. It was only later that they learned his history.

Perro Paco came to town once with a muleteer from the country, and finding, it would seem, city life more attractive than his former rural one, he allowed his master to go away without him, and took up his own residence in the capital. Left without a master, he showed himself quite able to take care of himself. He attached himself to the restaurant just mentioned, and always presented himself there at dinner-time, sure of a meal; for at first he was fed from kindness, and soon he became the pet of the establishment. Every day he had his dinner from the plate of some *habitué* of the place, and always honored this host by escorting him to his

PICADORS PREPARING FOR THE COMBAT.

house after the entertainment. He passed the day, after the usual manner of dogs, in wandering about the streets, or sleeping in sunny corners; but every evening he went regularly to the theatre, selecting different ones in turn, as if he had consulted the play bills. He walked down the theatre to a front seat in the pit, near the orchestra, where he listened always attentively to the scene on the stage, occasionally expressing his approval, or the reverse, with short barks, never loud enough to disturb the audience. A place was always made for him, and no alguazil would have dared to wound the susceptibility of the Madrileños by turning out their favorite.

On Sunday, he went regularly to the bull-fight, and one of the chief attractions there was Perro Paco watching the combat with the keenest interest, his own arrival greeted with applause, which he received modestly, always conducting himself with perfect decorum, and recognizing always the public approval with a dignified wag of the tail.

Perro Paco was the favorite of the hour. The walls were placarded with his portraits, a polka named for him, with his likeness on the outside sheet, sold readily. A daily newspaper called *El Perro Paco* professed to announce the opinions of the learned animal on every subject, especially political ones, thus making him the vehicle of all manner of squibs against the ruling ministry.

He was only a common cur, to tell the truth; smooth black, with white spots, though a certain distinction marked the way in which he wore his white shirt front. All the other black and white dogs came into notice on his account. "Is that Perro Paco?" was the question when they came into view.

Paco was but three years old when the Horners were in Madrid, and had enjoyed his fame less than a year. Alas! his career was a brief one, and he came to a tragic end.

The day the party left Madrid, one Monday morning in the train, which was crowded, their compartment was shared by two or three Spanish gentlemen diligently reading their morning papers as they whiffed away at cigarettes.

Mr. Horner had not found time in the hurry of packing, to open his newspaper; he was therefore surprised to hear one of the Spaniards say "Pobre Perro Paco!"

Bessie too, heard it, and could not resist an exclamation and an inquiry.

The gentleman, smiling, asked with a bad accent, "You read Spanish?" and handed her the paragraph. She read fluently enough to announce to the rest the sad information: Perro Paco had been mortally wounded at the bull-fight the day before.

It seemed that he became so interested in the contest, that he sprang down into the arena, and began to jump about the exasperated bull. The matador, either by accident, or because he was angry with the dog for interfering, jealous, perhaps, of the attention Perro Paco always drew to himself, wounded him in the side with his sharp weapon intended for the bull: Paco fell. The excitement was intense. Nobody cared what happened to the bull, or what became of the Espada. The poor wounded dog was put under the care of two or three skilful physicians. All the medical knowledge of Madrid was lavished on him, but in vain.

A FAIR SPECTATOR.

At the time of the paragraph Bessie read, Perro Paco was still living, but they heard the next day at Zaragoza, that the dog was dead.

He was permitted to lie in state for a few days, and it was said that crowds of people came to look at the dead form of the popular hero. Obituaries were written on him, poems composed in his honor, and his last will and testament was published; a document meant to be witty, and aiming at political reform.

In a few days, doubtless, he was forgotten, and some new plaything was amusing the volatile people of Madrid. Their devotion to Perro Paco, the enthusiasm for a dog which was universal throughout the capital, is a perfectly good illustration of the lightness and gayety of the Madrileños, or "Gatos de Madrid," as they call themselves.

The Espada, or matador, who puts the finishing touch to the *corrida*, by piercing the bull, is often a popular favorite; the hero of the hour. These men must possess great daring, a quick eye, firm wrist, and presence of mind. They are paid a large sum for each performance, besides the plaudits and bouquets of the audience. The matador, however, who slew the pet of the people, the admired Perro Paco, won for himself an unenviable fame. The Spaniards in the train were confident that his day was over; that he would never be able to face an audience or a bull again.

The Horners were as much surprised as any reader can be to find themselves all packed up, shawl-strapped, and again on their travels.

ORANGE BOY IN ARENA.

The fortnight in Madrid had gone like lightning, and it had nevertheless been long enough for them to do much sight-seeing, and to become greatly attached to the capital of Spain.

As for the Ricos, they were in despair to bid farewell to the friendly Americans; and the regret was mutual, for the worthy host had been so attentive, intelligent, and helpful, that they all came to regard him as a friend. The Horners long remembered as a kind of home, their long narrow rooms with large windows overlooking the Calle Mayor; with the bray of donkeys in the early morning, and later on, the music of the hand-organ, mingled with the heavier noises of the street, — the pleasant almuerzos and comidas about the round table in their small dining-room, served by the ever-anxious Rico, who watched every mouthful, to see if the señoras were satisfied with the food, and the quiet evenings around their lamp, when, tired after standing about in the gallery, or a long succession of armories and royal stables, they talked or wrote letters, mended the now much deteriorated toilets, and consulted maps and guide-books as to the rest of their course.

Before they left Madrid, it was quite settled that Philip should join them at Zaragoza; and this was the one prospect that cheered them in breaking up their establishment. The packing was something fearful, so many photographs, books, Spanish mantas and hats had to be now finally disposed of in trunks.

OUTSIDE VIEW OF THE ARENA.

CHAPTER XXXVI.

NAPOLEON IN SPAIN.

CHARLES THE THIRD.

SPAIN, after Philip the Fifth, was governed by three of his sons in succession, the last of whom, Charles the Third, held the throne until 1788. He was a prince of considerable talent, excellent intentions, and blameless morals, and through his ministers, he introduced the country to a degree of prosperity to which it had been unused since the days of Philip the Second.

His son Charles the Fourth succeeded him, but he, unlike his father, was more weak and pitiful than any sovereign of the age.

Spain had no part in the French Revolution at the end of the eighteenth century, but it was now about to become the theatre of events that opened a new world of hope to Europe. Napoleon, who had been passing from conquest to conquest, after the battle of Jena, in which the Prussian army, opposed to him, had been annihilated, now turned his attention to Spain.

The crown-prince Ferdinand, and his father, the king, were at enmity with each other. Each sought the aid, or at least the sympathy, of Napoleon, most unwisely; for such communications gave that wily manager a pretext for intervention he had long desired. It was universally believed he had espoused the cause of the prince; and this view was a popular one, for the queen, his mother, was especially hated by the Spanish. Thus the French gradually entered the peninsula without exciting suspicion. The king and court, terrified, took flight from Madrid, seeing before them otherwise the fate of Louis the Sixteenth, who delayed too long. The king published a decree abdicating in favor of his son.

MONUMENT OF THE DOS DE MAYO.

But this was not what Napoleon wanted. By his orders, Murat was already on his way to Madrid to assume command, and it did not suit his plan that the Spaniards should themselves settle their difficulty. The French troops entered Madrid, and Ferdinand, relying on their countenance, made his solemn entry into the capital, but again unwisely was persuaded to leave Madrid and go to Bayonne to meet the emperor, never dreaming but that he was to be recognized by this powerful ally as the legitimate successor of Charles the Fourth, instead of which, after a gloomy dinner of state, the unfortunate prince was informed that he, too, must renounce the crown of Spain.

Meantime there was open insurrection in the capital. The populace broke out, and French soldiers were attacked and killed. But

DRIVING THE BULLS DOWN.

the vengeance of Murat was swift. The insurgents were overpowered, and numbers of citizens shot in cold blood. This was on the twentieth of May, 1808, and an obelisk called El dos de Mayo commemorates the gallant resistance of the people under two leaders, Daoiz and Velarde, who there won the name the first heroes of Spanish independence. When Ferdinand, who was still at Bayonne, heard this, he yielded, and resigned the crown, and for a couple of country houses, and two life annuities, the crown of Spain and the Indies was renounced in favor of Napoleon, by both father and son.

The Spanish nation was not inclined to submit; the country was thrown into tumult. On all sides the population declared war on Napoleon, and called upon England for assistance; but Joseph Bonaparte was brought from Naples to receive the crown, and divisions of the French army sent against the insurgents in all directions. They were entirely routed at Baylen, and Sir Arthur Wellesley (afterwards the Duke of Wellington) landed in Portugal with English troops to help the Spanish.

At this time Napoleon himself was occupied elsewhere; but at the beginning of November, 1808, he crossed the Pyrénées,

VELARDE AND DAOIZ.

to examine more closely the victories of the Spaniards. In December he marched against the forces of Sir John Moore, who had entered Spain from Portugal with an English army, but who was forced now to retreat. He was pursued by Soult, with a body of French troops, and attacked at Corunna. The French were defeated, but Moore fell at the moment of his victory. Every child knows the "Burial of Sir John Moore." He was buried in haste, for the English ships were waiting to take the troops, and it was unsafe to delay, as the French were close at hand with numbers far superior.

Napoleon now thought the Spanish matter was settled, and left Spain, with his brother Joseph in possession of the capital. But before this great general had been many weeks in Paris, reports reached him of continued insubordination.

The city of Zaragoza had successfully resisted its besiegers in the

THE ESPADA.

summer of 1808, and early the next year its walls were stormed in from different places, according to the ordinary precedents of war.

THE ARENA.

The place was now in possession of the French, but the besiegers found on the contrary that their work was only begun.

The streets were trenched and barricaded. Every dwelling was converted into a fortress, and for many days the French were forced to besiege house by house. The inhabitants had no organized army, and the people would obey no one but some stout peasants chosen by themselves, and Palafox, a young officer of the king's body-guard. The city was mad with patriotism and hatred of the French, and there was singing and dancing in the streets. The Maid of Zaragoza, a very pretty girl, named Agustina, only twenty-two years of age, fought side by side with her lover, and when he fell, mortally wounded, worked his cannon herself. Wilkie has painted her portrait, and Byron has sung her fame.

The brave city had to surrender at last. On the twentieth of February, what was left of Zaragoza capitulated, for no attempt was made to relieve it. In other places the Spanish were beaten, and it appeared as if the subjugation of the Spanish peninsula must become complete.

Had the Emperor himself taken up the command, this would have probably been the case; but he was elsewhere occupied in arms, and with his second marriage to Marie Louise. Moreover, Wellington was unlike any of the generals whom Napoleon had before encountered. In July, 1812, after many successes and reverses, Wellington marched upon Madrid. King Joseph fled, and, although this was not the end, it was the beginning of it. In 1813 Spain was rid of her enemies. In June Wellington won the famous battle of Vittoria, and ended the contest. A year later the power of Napoleon everywhere was over.

The Bourbon dynasty both in France and Spain was restored, and Ferdinand the Seventh was reinstated. But as we have seen in the course of this period of agitation, the Spanish people had gained ideas of more independence in government, and the ancient arbitrary rule of monarchs and favorites was forever at an end.

"How do you think your Napoleon appears now, papa?" asked

Bessie, after they had been reviewing these things, in connection with Zaragoza, which they were fast approaching in the train.

"Still as a great man, my dear, and a wonderfully interesting one."

In Egypt, the Horners had seen the battle-fields where Bonaparte undertook to establish the rule of France, — in Berlin the trophies returned which he had carried off, — at Jena, the scene of one of his most signal triumphs.

"But everywhere, papa, we see the destruction caused by his troops; and if you wish to see the art treasures of the countries he has conquered, you must go to the Louvre."

"That sounds, Bessie, as if it came out of a guide-book!" said Miss Lejeune; "and as for the pictures, Spain has succeeded better than other countries in protecting her treasures."

Bessie blushed a little, and admitted that she only said it to tease papa. "But the French generals did carry off quantities of things from the churches, and blew up fortresses everywhere."

After the battle of Vittoria, the French fled in disorder, Joseph himself riding a mule. It is said that nearly two thousand vehicles were collected behind the town containing the plunder of the French army during the five years on the Peninsula; and when Joseph's own carriage was seized, it was gorged with stolen goods. Some cabinet pictures belonging to the royal family thus came into the hands of the Duke of Wellington, and afterwards adorned the walls of Apsley house; and it may be supposed that the English were not behindhand in taking their share of the spoils, deeming it now fairly theirs by right of conquest.

The Horners were now fairly on their way out of Spain, as Zaragoza was to be one of their last halting places. This journey, to their great satisfaction, could be made by daylight, and it proved a pleasant contrast to the last weary jaunt from Jaen to Madrid, when they were tired and dusty from their long morning in the diligence. They were now fresh and wide awake, and enjoyed the scenery from the windows, though it seems tame after the glowing soil of Andalusia, and the abrupt passes of the Sierra Nevada.

CARRYING OFF THE VICTIM.

They were now in Aragon, the kingdom of Ferdinand and his ancestors, joined, at his marriage with Isabella, to Castile. The native dress is somewhat different from that of other parts of Spain. Knee breeches of cotton velvet ornamented with filagree buttons were worn by the men, and short black velvet waistcoats, showing the wide girdle or faja below, which holds all sorts of things, like a pocket. The panuelas worn by men and women upon their heads, were tied about the forehead like a band, leaving the top of the head uncovered.

END OF THE CONTEST.

CHAPTER XXXVII.

PHILIP'S ADVENTURES.

ARMS OF ZARAGOZA.

"ARE you really here, dear Philip, safe and sound?" demanded Miss Lejeune, as she looked him carefully over, to make sure with her own eyes that she had hold of the right boy.

"Safe and sound, aunt Dut, and glad to be here, for your night trains are tiresome work."

Philip was sitting on a sofa in their hotel room at Zaragoza, with Miss Lejeune on one side of him and Bessie on the other. Mr. Horner sat opposite, and Tommy leaned on the railing of the window.

"How you have grown, my dear!" continued Miss Lejeune. "How could you do it in two months?"

"Nonsense, Miss Lejeune," he replied. "It is only because you have forgotten how I look. Measure, papa, will you? I was not quite up to you when we parted."

They stood up, back to back, close together. Philip was perceptibly taller than his father, though his shoulder did not reach the broader line of his stouter parent's back.

"Altogether, he looks different, however," said Bessie, eying him critically.

"Come, I won't stand this!" he exclaimed, half laughing and

half annoyed. "I am as hungry as a bear, and don't fancy this close inspection."

The fact was, he had grown, and had gained an air of manliness and self-reliance which changed him. His hair was thick, and rather longer than he usually wore it. Tommy was secretly a little afraid of him.

The Horners had arrived at Zaragoza the evening before, and had gone at once to the hotel agreed upon, half expecting to find Philip there before them. On the contrary, there was no sign of him, and the most careful inquiry failed to reveal him; — they all remembered a time when they were to meet in a hotel at Cologne, and remained hidden from each other for several hours.

LUZ.

There was no cause for anxiety, because the time and hour of arrival had not been absolutely fixed; and they went to bed full of hope for the morning, Miss Lejeune and Bessie in two little dark bedrooms, opening by glass doors upon the salon, and the others in another room near by. Still Mr. Horner was greatly relieved to be aroused about seven, the next morning, by a good sharp knock at his door, and a well-known voice, saying:

"Mr. Horner?— Papa, are you here?"

The door was instantly open to him, and a very merry reception ensued, as the costumes of the hosts were not full dress.

"I recognized your boots, sir, at once, at the door, and knew there could be no mistake."

Mr. Horner's boots were well known to his family, for he had a theory about his feet which caused him to wear them of an individual type, with which they were all familiar.

Philip had been travelling by rail from Huesca, the farthest point on the railway line which will one day make a new route over the Pyrénées with France. The ladies were aroused by the welcome knocking and laughter next door, and soon all were ready and waiting for their coffee to be brought, and something more substantial for Philip.

Question followed question. They were all impatient to know Phil's experiences, and yet too full of their own news to keep silent themselves, until Mr. Horner said, "Come, now, begin regularly and tell your adventures.

"How did you get on, my dear," asked Miss Lejeune, "in those wild places where they speak no French?"

"Why, I can speak Spanish," said Philip with a sly smile.

"What!" they all exclaimed. "You speak Spanish?"

"Do not be so set up about your own accomplishments," replied he; and as the waiter entered opportunely at that moment with the tray, he very coolly gave in Spanish all the necessary directions for what was lacking, and asked the proper questions about the time of almuerzo, etc., with as much ease as any of them could have shown. The others gazed amazed, and Bessie said, "Philip, what's this?"

"Oh! I picked it up; don't you worry. Besides, if you keep asking me questions, I shall never get on." As he spoke, he helped himself to a very nice-looking omelette, while Miss Augusta was preparing coffee for the rest.

"Tommy, you may have half my omelette," Philip went on. "If I eat this chop beside, I shall do."

"Well!" said Mr. Horner, and "Well!" said all the rest. Philip then began, and gave, not without interruptions and exclamations from the rest, the account of his wonderful crossing of the Pyrénées.

"In the first place," he said, "you have no idea yet how lovely it is at Luz; such a pretty valley, shut in by hills, with distant peaks filling the gap where it opens, and our robber castle overlooking the town. Mamma and Mary came with me up to the Cirque de Gavarnie, which is a wonderful place,— an amphitheatre

CIRQUE DE GAVARNIE.

of immense rocks, snow covered, and a waterfall dropping down the steep precipice. It is one of the sights in the Pyrénées, and we had seen it at a great distance from a peak we went up on donkeys."

"You wrote about that," said Tommy.

"Don't interrupt!" said Bessie, giving him a thump with her elbow.

"From the road as you approached the Cirque," continued Philip, "can be seen up high against the sky, the Brêche de Roland "—

"I know!" cried Bessie, "which he cut with one hack of his sword Durendal"—

"Don't interrupt!" retorted Tommy, returning her thump with interest.

"Well, through that breach I determined to go," said Philip; "and although people wagged their heads and said it was impossible, I managed to accomplish it, and what was more, to persuade mamma it was the same thing as going in a horse-car.

"You must know I had been cramming Spanish to fill up my time at Luz, and there is a good old Spaniard in the hotel who loves to talk with us. Mary does it in French; but I soon got to risking my Castellano, and he was delighted. The donkey women and men talk a vile *patois*,— a queer mixture of French and Spanish, and Basque, for aught I knew,— and I picked up a good deal of that, which was lucky; for by talking with them at Gavarnie, I found out there was a Spanish guide who was coming back into Spain, and who knew the pass through the Brèche de Roland perfectly well."

"How splendid!" murmured Bessie, and again was nudged by Tommy.

"I shall say splendid," said Bessie, "that is not interrupting."

"Splendid it was!" exclaimed Philip; "I never enjoyed anything so much. The guide's name was Manuel Molina, and he was excellent. He talks a little English, and knows everything. We started early in the morning from the little house in the Cirque; then we crossed the stream that makes the waterfall, and it was like flies walking on the side of a wall after that, only there was a path.

"The breach itself is a narrow passage between those high walls, nearly a quarter of a mile, and then we came out on the Spanish side, and could see away off into Aragon!

"By and by we had a superb view of the Mont Perdu, the highest peak but two of the Pyrénées. It is in Spain, and with its two connected peaks, is called Las tres Hermanas. Then we went on and reached a little place called Gaulis, where there is a cabin, very comfortable, and a most friendly Spanish shepherd. There we spent the night, and I tell you I was tired.

"The next day we came down to Boucharo, and after that, it is a very easy walk by a lake, to a hideous place called the Baths of Panticosa. I could not bear the thought of stopping there for an instant. It is all built up with hotels and pretentious fountains, like a water-cure establishment, which it is. Luckily I found there was a good road down to Jaca, and we got horses and rode to it that night. My guide left me there to go back into France over the new diligence route. It was Saturday night, and at first we thought we should have to sleep in the streets, for the little town was crowded, on account of a *fiesta*, for the whole country round. Everybody gabbling Spanish, but just as friendly and hospitable as possible; so that I was glad that I had to stay over Sunday, although that is why I did not arrive here sooner. There was a grand procession with delegations from every village, each bearing its own standard. Bishops, in their robes, stiff with gold, images, and relics of Saint Orosia, and dancing boys with castanets, who danced backwards in the procession, quite like those Arabs, Bessie, at Jerusalem."

"Dervishes," corrected Bessie.

"The crowd," continued Philip, "was just as interesting as the procession; for different villages have different costumes. Bright purple seemed the prevailing color for sashes; but there was every gaudy tint imaginable swarming in the streets. If you've been

A RELAY.

seeing these things all the time, you must have had a wild experience."

"All days are not Saints' days," said Mr. Horner. "And I fancy you have seen something different from any of our wonders."

"Monday night I came away from my dear little Jaca. It is a walled town, Bessie; we walked all around it at sunset."

"Who was we?"

"The landlord Mor; just the nicest man you ever saw. Our conversation was rather limited, but he seemed to enjoy my Spanish!"

"He must be exactly like Rico!" they exclaimed.

Philip came from Jaca to Huesca by a diligence, much like that which brought the others from Grenada to Jaen. He was perched up in the cupé, where he slept a little, but woke occasionally, to see the moon lighting the drowsy towns through which they passed. At Huesca, a stupid, glaring town, he had to wait all day; but he was so sleepy, a bed and quiet was all he demanded of the place; after which he came on by rail, and reached Zaragoza as we have seen, early in the following morning.

CHAPTER XXXVIII.

ZARAGOZA.

WITH added zest on account of Philip's arrival, the Horners set about sight-seeing in Zaragoza. There are two cathedrals to be visited, one of which is very ancient, a severe and sombre pile, which dates back 290 A. D. The other, the Cathedral del Pilar, is a modern gaudy edifice, but it is the favorite church of the natives, on account of the legend connected with it. Tradition says that the apostle Santiago, after the Crucifixion, came to Spain, to preach the Gospel. When he had reached Zaragoza, in his sleep he was visited by a celestial vision. The Virgin appeared standing on a jasper pillar surrounded by angels, and spoke to him, saying she wished to have a chapel built on that very spot. Santiago hastened to fulfil her bidding, and erected a small chapel, which, it is said, was often visited by the Holy Mother. The present cathedral was built in the place of the ancient one about two centuries ago, with all the lack of taste belonging to that period. In the Sacred Chapel is the Holy Image with the pillar, concealed by a heavy cloth, and enclosed in a silver railing. Jasper pillars support the cupola, and this is hung about with old banners captured from the Moors. There is a small room beneath, reached by some descending steps where the heart of Don John of Austria, the hero of Lepanto, is kept.

In the security of this holy chapel is preserved all that remains of the treasure of the Virgin, — gifts made to her shrine by devotees. There are still many ornaments of pearls and diamonds, and mantles embroidered and enriched with gold; but the French carried away the greater part of these treasures.

The Horners especially wanted to see the leaning tower. They walked about the streets looking for it in vain, until they began to feel as if all the steeples in town were out of the perpendic-

THE LEANING TOWER.

ular. The principal streets of Zaragoza are broad, and ornamented with large squares; but the less inportant ones are narrow and winding, so that it is impossible to see any great distance. Having passed the morning in studying the two cathedrals, and wandering about the streets, they took a fresh start towards sunset, and with full directions from the hotel, soon found themselves below the leaning tower, which did lean in an alarming manner, for as they stood beneath it, it seemed as if it must come tottering down. But there it has stood, firmly planted, since the beginning of the sixteenth century, although it is called the Torre Nueva, or new tower. It was built by Spanish and Moorish architects, combining their skill. It inclines like the leaning tower of Pisa, but not so much as that.

The tower is on a large square, and there is a little house at the foot of it, where was a very hospitable and friendly concierge, or guardian of the tower, who urged our party to ascend to the top.

Miss Lejeune, as usual, demurred. She found the excellent wooden chair in the shade too comfortable to leave, when she was told there were two hundred and sixty steps to go up.

But the children begged her to come.

"Think, aunt Dut," said Tommy, "our last tower in Spain!"

"And my first," added Philip.

"Well, I suppose I must," she said, starting from her seat with energy, as the boy who had been sent for the keys approached. An iron door was unlocked, and they set out upon the weary winding stairs within the tower. A stray dog joined the expedition and kept with the party all the way.

The view from the top is extensive and fine, and Miss Augusta after she had recovered her breath, was enthusiastic. It was very windy, and the platform seemed to waver. There are strong railings across the open arched spaces, and it is perfectly safe, but the party all felt a little insecure. The dog evidently felt so too. He sat very meek in the shelter of one of the arches, and was all ready to go down with the rest as soon as the general move was made.

"But where is the Maid?" asked Philip, as they were walking back to the hotel. They saw nothing of her, and there is little or no trace left of the long-sustained siege. There is indeed little to see of ancient splendor. Though the houses in the old streets are built with massive masonry, and there are patios with solid columns, and remains of fine carving, now used as warehouses and receptacles for old rubbish.

The ancient kingdom of Aragon is now divided into three provinces, of which that of Zaragoza is one. Formerly, its nucleus in the heart of the Spanish Pyrénées, was the refuge of the routed Goths. Here in time petty states arose, from which Aragon grew to be a kingdom. Catalonia became a part of it in the twelfth century, and later, when Ferdinand was married to Isabella, it was joined to Castile. The Aragonese have been remarkable in history for their love of independ-

OLD COURT-YARD.

ence and public liberty. One of their early laws was to the effect that "whenever the king should infringe the powers, any other might be elected in his stead, even should he be a Pagan."

The hotel at Zaragoza was upon a large square, which, in the evening, was filled with people chatting upon benches, walking up and down in the warm summer air; and here and there voices arose, softly singing light music. The Horners sat in the window of their room, without candles, watching the scene below, but

OX TEAM OF ARAGON.

more interested in talking with Philip, and comparing notes of the different experiences of the family since its members had been separated.

"Only think, Philip," said Tommy, "that you did not see Hubert Vaughan!"

"I know," replied Philip; "he was a nice fellow, was he not?"

THE COLEGIO DE PROCURADORES, ZARAGOZA.

"First-rate," replied Tommy. "I miss him all the time."

"My mother thought you had lost your mind when she first heard that you had adopted, as it were, a large family," said Philip, turning to his father.

Mr. Horner laughed. "It was rash," he said, "but it all turned out very well, in spite of the sad ending. I pity Hubert. He is a fine little fellow, and his life now at Gibraltar must be sad and dull."

"Mr. Hervey thinks he has met Colonel Vaughan," said Philip.

"Mr. Hervey! Why, he was gone long before we met the Vaughans," said Miss Lejeune.

"Oh! Did not you know he had come back from America?" asked Philip. "He only went over to see his mother for a minute or so in Boston, and came right back."

"Back to Luz!" demanded Miss Lejeune, sitting up and leaning forward to examine Philip's face as he heard the question.

"No, not yet," replied Philip, with a half laugh; "but there is constant writing, and that was one reason why I did not mind leaving mamma and Mary. Hervey is sure to turn up before they have to go away."

Philip stood up, put his hands in his pockets, and walked to the other window. Miss Augusta made a movement to follow him, and began "Philip," but changed her mind, and leaned back again in her seat. There was a little silence, broken only by her favoite ejaculation in an undertone, "Well! well!"

The silence was broken by something very like a snore from Tommy, who had been sitting on the floor with his head against Bessie's chair. He roused himself, and said, "I believe I am a little sleepy, and I will go to bed."

The early start caused by Philip's arrival in the morning, and a long day of sight-seeing, was quite enough to account for his condition.

"There was a party at Jaca," said Philip, "that I think must have been Americans, although I did not speak to them; a gentleman and two ladies, one rather elderly, and a young girl.

They sketched, which made me think they were English at first. I saw them in the morning. All were sitting on the edge of a field, and painting the walls of the town with Oroel the mountain, behind. I wish we could go back there some day. You have no idea how pretty it is. Jaca is an important little town. There is a cathedral there, very ancient; and it was the scene of a battle with the Moors, about the end of the eighth century. The women fought with the men; they have a sham fight now every year to celebrate the day, when the women go out and fight."

"How about those sketching-people, Philip; did the young girl have light hair?"

"Yes; in a braid down her back. I think they were staying to see the fiesta, for they went off the next morning very early in a delightful little omnibus, all by themselves, to cross the Pyrénées by the new diligence road. I heard the noise of their departure, and put my head out of the window. There was the landlord and his daughter, and the maids, all running, speeding the parting guest. I never saw so much hand-baggage. They had shawl straps, and those flat things you see all over Spain."

"Alforcas!" said Bessie.

"Yes; and drawing-boards, and lunch-baskets"—

"And a india rubber waterproof!" said a small voice in the distance. Tommy was standing in the doorway, with one shoe in his hand and none on his feet.

"I came back to get my other shoe," he explained.

"But how do you know about the waterproof?" cried Philip.

"What mark was there on the boxes?" said Bessie.

"I don't know; I did not see the baggage very well."

"It must be, of course it was, the other H's," said Bessie.

Pretty soon the party broke up, and they all went to bed, as sleepy as Tommy; but after Bessie was quiet, with her head on the pillow, Miss Lejeune lingered still, leaning on the balcony, in the soft night air.

Finally she turned away, closed the window, put out the lights, murmuring to herself with a smile, "Well! well!"

CATHEDRAL, BARCELONA.

CHAPTER XXXIX.

BARCELONA.

IN twenty-four hours the Horners had left Zaragoza, and after another long railroad journey, had reached Barcelona, passing across the province of Catalonia, one of the most individual of the divisions of Spain. The Catalans are a strongly marked race, differing from all other Spaniards. As they live on the border lands between Spain and France, they have in all periods of disagreements wavered from one side to the other; in their hearts and souls they consider themselves neither Spaniards nor French, but simply Catalans. They are industrious, business-like and enterprising; they have been called the Scotch of the country; honest, thrifty, and sober, with an immense sense of their own superiority and contempt for their neighbors; a feeling justified by the fact that they hold the commerce of Spain in their hands.

The dress of the Catalans is perhaps less picturesque than that of other provinces. The chief distinction is a cotton night-cap-shaped *gorro*, sometimes purple, but generally red; for red is the prevailing Catalan color. The oxen are oddly decorated with high humps on their yokes gayly ornamented.

Catalonia was called the Spanish March, or frontier, at the time when the French took possession of it, after driving out the Moors in the eighth century. Under one of the governors it revolted, and the counts of Barcelona remained independent from the ninth to the twelfth centuries. This was its greatest period of wealth and prosperity, and it is the tradition of this power which makes the descendants of this free people such troublesome subjects.

As we have seen, Catalonia was, by marriage, merged in the

crown of Aragon. It thus lost the name, though not the spirit, of independence; by the time of Ferdinand and Isabella, when it

CATALONIA CART.

became, of course, a part of Castile, it possessed neither the prosperity nor the power of ancient days.

Always rebellious, it has been found on the side opposed to the king on the throne in every revolution. Always obliged to surrender, it is to this day ever ready for civil war and revolution.

Barcelona, its chief place, is the second largest city in Spain. It is very happily placed on the shores of the Mediterranean, and its climate, mild in winter, is agreeable at all seasons. Washington Irving had occasion to visit it while he was American minister in Spain, in order to present an official letter to the young Queen Isabella, then not more than fifteen years old. He was delighted with the city, in contrast to the less favored situation of Madrid, and describes living there as the very poetry of existence.

Barcelona comes into English history at the time of the war of the Spanish succession, 1701-14, when English, Dutch and Austrians combined to resist Louis the Fourteenth in his plan of making his grandson, Philip, king of Spain.

While Marlborough was fighting in this cause in the Netherlands, the English sent an expedition to Spain under Lord Peterborough, one of the most extraordinary characters that ever lived, brilliant, courageous, but eccentric to the last degree. The task assigned to him was to attack Barcelona, a difficult one, for the city on one side is protected by the sea, on the other by strong fortifications.

Peterborough conceived the idea of a bold attack upon this forttress, and by night, with a little army, he approached the walls of Monjuich. Here they halted till daybreak, when the enemy came into the outer ditch to meet them. This was what the English were prepared for. They rushed forward, put the Spaniards to flight, and entered the works together with the fugitives. Before the garrison had recovered from their surprise, Peterborough was master of the outworks. He was aided by reinforcements, and the fortress soon fell. Barcelona followed, and Peterborough had the glory of taking, with a handful of men, one of the largest and strongest towns of Europe.

In spite of the successes of the Arch-duke Charles, the Austrian competitor for Spain, it was the Bourbon prince who gained the throne. By the close of 1707, Catalonia was the only part of Spain which still adhered to Charles; and six years afterwards, the peace of Utrecht put an end to this conflict of the nations, a peace which the poor Catalans alone had real reason to regret.

They had been the faithful allies of England throughout the struggle, and England should have made the liberties of Catalonia a condition of peace; but Queen Anne and the English contented themselves with an empty promise of good offices to secure

PRISON OF INQUISITION, BARCELONA.

them. The unhappy people, abandoned by those whom they had so faithfully served, refused to accept the conditions offered by the Bourbon King of Spain, and continued in arms, hoping for outside help. Barcelona was blockaded. The resistance lasted more than a year. The insurgents hung up over the high altar of their cathedral the solemn declaration of the Queen of England to protect them. But the struggle of course was hopeless. No aid came from the outside. A great part of the city was reduced to ashes, and at last Barcelona was taken by storm. Many of the inhabitants were imprisoned or transported, and the ancient privileges of Catalonia for which they had fought so valiantly, were finally abolished.

The Horners had a couple of days to wait at Barcelona before taking the steamer which runs once a week between that port at Marseilles. They had time to see pretty much all the sights of the town; the prison of the Inquisition, now robbed of its terrors, but for years filled with the victims of the cruel rule of the Spanish church, the fortress built by Philip the Fifth, to have command over the city, and especially over the Castle of Monjuich, surprised by Peterborough, from the summit of which there is a magnificent view, as the fort is seven hundred and fifty-two feet above the level of the sea.

GIGANTS.

The Catalans are still fond of show and parade. While the Horners were there they saw the streets crowded to witness a pageant of a solemn nature, a funeral procession, when the dignitaries of the church marched solemnly, bearing banners. It was accompanied by solemn music, and very impressive. The valet de place who took them about the first day, told them they ought to stay to a *fiesta* soon to take place, when the *Gigants* would be carried about the streets.

"He means giants," said Bessie to Philip in a low tone; "that is what Juan used to call them."

The gigants, as described in the imperfect English of the guide, would seem to be some traditional heroes of the Catalans, thus honored in a rude fashion.

The cathedral is sober and harmonious. It is Gothic and belongs mostly to the best and purest period. It is approached by an elevated flight of steps. The belfry towers are lofty, dating from the end of the fourteenth century, when the whole cathedral was finished, except the portions which still remain incomplete, like the principal façade. The interior is dark, solemn, and imposing, and the stained windows are among the finest in Spain, dating between the fourteen and fifteen hundreds. In

THE BATTLE OF LEPANTO.

one of the chapels is a crucifix called Cristo de Lepanto, which was carried on the prow of the flagship of Don Juan of Austria, at the battle of Lepanto, fought against the Moors in 1571, by Spain, Venice and Austria.

It is bent sideways, because, according to the legend, as the Moors directed their guns against the sacred image, it turned away, and thus avoided the infidel bullet.

They had not allowed themselves time to go out to the Monastery of Montserrat, an excursion which requires a day at least, and better two. It is one of the celebrated shrines in Spain, and is still visited yearly by numbers of pilgrims. It is the subject of many legends and superstitions, and the treasure of the Virgin enshrined there was once immense. The French carried off most of it, and when the French troops were garrisoned there the place was almost destroyed. The former church and monastery no longer exist; the modern convent, built by the orders of Ferdinand the Seventh, in 1827, overlooks a broad and magnificent view.

The Horners were content to wander about the streets of Barcelona, enjoying the soft breezes from the sea, and awaiting now with some impatience, the steamer which would so soon bring them to join their mother and sister.

Yet Bessie sighed to be leaving charming Spain, and Miss Lejeune did it with regret. The chief dream of her life, as she declared, was now coming to an end, and what more had she to look forward to!

The chief street of Barcelona is called the Rambla, a broad boulevard, or succession of them, filled in the warm evening with people strolling up and down. There are also Paseos and public gardens, where the people can enjoy out-door life, in the shade of large trees, and with fountains cooling the air.

Our party lingered in the open air quite late on their last evening in Barcelona. It was their last evening also in Spain, and they wished to enjoy it to the full.

The next morning they had to be up betimes, for no one was quite sure at what hour the steamer would leave. There was not much packing to do, for they had not been long enough in the place to establish the air of comfortable confusion which usually distinguished their hotel rooms. The chief part of their luggage had been forwarded direct to Paris from Madrid, and since they left the capital they had been travelling with very little encumbrance. So they walked from the hotel to the port, followed by a hand-cart containing their effects, descended the long, handsome steps of the jetty, and put forth in a little boat to their steamer.

CHAPTER XL.

OUT OF SPAIN.

DELAYS, as usual in Spain, were numerous, and it was noon before the steamer was fairly off. The party of Americans established themselves comfortably in the stern of the ship, well tucked in with rugs, for the air of the sea was fresh as soon as they lost the influence of land breezes. Lovely indeed was the receding shore, the hills rising behind the town in jagged peaks, dotted here and there with houses. The water of the Mediterranean sparkled and danced, and the sky was clear and almost cloudless.

They all looked long and wistfully back upon the country in which they had enjoyed so much.

"I suppose, Bessie," said Philip, beginning to banter her upon her historical streak, "that you are well versed in the history of Spain; you have it, so to speak, at your fingers' ends?"

"Fairly well," replied Bessie, not without some vanity, or at least self-confidence.

"Let me see," said Philip. "The Goths had something to do with it, did they not? They got it away from the Romans, under a man named Roderick. Was he the same as the Cid?"

"Philip, you are very funny," said Bessie scornfully; "I know you are really dying to know all about it; if not, you will do well not to goad me on, for I shall begin at the very beginning and expound the whole course of events to you."

"Give me the guide-book," said Philip, yawning, "and I will look it through. I dare say in half an hour I shall catch up with you in knowledge of the Spanish kings."

ARMS OF BARCELONA.

Bessie shook her head. "You just wait till you have tried it; the minute you begin to find out anything about it, you will perceive that you know nothing at all."

"If Philip will retire and study the guide-book for half an hour, as he says," remarked Mr. Horner, "we will then hold an examination and see which knows the most, Philip or Bessie."

"Very well," replied Bessie with alacrity; "only I should like to look at the book once."

"Not fair, not fair!" cried Philip, holding it out of her reach.

"Oh, it's of no consequence," she returned with dignity, "I was

MONTSERRAT.

not quite sure whether Pelayo was seven hundred and eighteen or seven hundred and twenty."

"Don't be alarmed, Bessie," said Miss Lejeune, "for if you are one of the examined, none of the rest of us know enough how to conduct the case."

"True enough," replied Philip, touched by Bessie's imperturbable good nature; "and on the whole, I much prefer to have Bessie know for all of us, and to remain ignorant myself. Do you know, Bessie," he continued, looking her all over, "I really believe, now, that you will never become a prig!"

"Really, Philip," she retorted, with a toss of her head, "how do you feel about yourself in that regard?"

Philip pulled something that would sometime become a mustache, and said:

"Let us change the subject;" and thus ended the passage-at-arms.

Not long after they were summoned below to a mid-day meal, which was not almuerzo, but more like a regular dinner.

"No puchero!" exclaimed Bessie.

"Glad of it!" said Tommy. "It is the first day we have not had to eat it since we came to Spain."

Tommy had spent the last hour in visiting the live stock on board. There were quite a number of passengers, all talking French. The stewards were French, and there was an indescribable absence of everything Spanish, although a few of the sailors were Catalans, and wore hanging red caps.

LIVE STOCK.

Alas, the Spanish campaign was over, and all Spanish sights, sounds (and, shall we say, smells?) were rapidly disappearing. It was too soon to change the current of their thoughts, and their minds kept reverting to their Spanish life. Words in Castellano came readily to their lips, even before the French ones required for the moment.

"As for my Italian," said Miss Lejeune, "I fear it is lost forever. I think of *siempre* and *tiempo*, instead of *sempre* and *tempo*, whenever I try to turn an Italian sentence."

"You will pick it up again;" said Bessie; "and I must learn it, for, papa dear, I am now very anxious to go to Naples and Sicily. You know Gonsalvo de Cordova was there" —

"That, of course, is the best of reasons," began Philip.

"My daughter," said Mr. Horner, "do not mention any more countries to me. I am going HOME now, and I mean to settle down this time. I begin to feel a little too old for so much travelling, and I want to make acquaintance once more with my own chimney-corner."

"Too old! what nonsense, papa! but I will not press the question. You have been a most obedient parent, and since we can have our own house this winter, I have no objection to going home. But remember; we are never to settle down for good. The Horners must always be a roving family."

"You young people," said the long-suffering parent with a deep-drawn sigh, "I dare say, will be ready to start off again; but I think your mother and I, after this, will stay at home and content ourselves with letters. Is that your opinion, Augusta?"

Miss Lejeune shook her head. She was indeed an inveterate traveller. Nevertheless she said:

"I want to go home now, and see what there really is in my boxes. Let me see, we left one at Madrid; I sent two to London, from Bordeaux, and there is that one at Paris that came from Beirût, with all my Eastern things in it. Bessie, I mean to have that red and white Cairo blanket for a portière in my bedroom."

Thus it will be seen that even she had her mind turned towards America. The party was to join Mrs. Horner and Mary at Marseilles, where it was hoped they were already waiting impatiently. All were to go at once to England. It was now the beginning of July, and they expected to pass the summer months at the lakes, perhaps going into Scotland in September. It will be remembered that the Horner family had as yet no experience of the charms of English scenery.

The plan was to reach New York about the first of October, and to go at once upon arriving home for their own house was now vacant. Miss Lejeune's rooms were always ready for her, under lock and key.

"But oh! the joy of seeing Mary so soon," cried Bessie.

"Do you really think, Philip, that Mr. Hervey is there with them?" asked Miss Lejeune.

"I should not wonder," he replied with a mysterious smile.

In thus talking over their past experiences and future plans, they found the time pass rapidly. After dinner they watched a superb sunset, for many clouds had come up and were piled tumultuously about the west; the wind too was rising, and as they were now far out from land, there was more motion than they liked. Little heeding it, however, they all bade each other good-night and went below early, Miss Lejeune and Bessie to a snug little cabin which they luckily had all to themselves.

Luckily, for about midnight a violent storm came up. The ship rolled and tossed, the rain poured down in sheets upon the deck.

In the state-room the two ladies were both awake, for everything was on the loose. They had not thought to take the usual precautions to secure their effects, as it was the only night, and had seemed so calm when they went to bed.

"Bessie, are you awake?" asked Miss Lejeune.

"I should think so," she replied.

"What is that rolling about on the floor?" asked her companion.

"I can see my boots and your hat, and all our clothes, sliding about," said Bessie, putting her head out and looking down from her dizzy height.

"But that round thing that bangs — there it goes again!" she cried, as the ship rolled again.

"I'm afraid it's the water pitcher; we must have left it on the floor!"

"O Heaven!" cried Miss Lejeune in dismay, "then everything is wet down there."

PORT AT MARSEILLES.

"Everything is wet up here," retorted Bessie, "for the port-hole is not tight, and each wave splashes in!"

"My dear child, you had better come down and lie on the sofa!"

"I will come down and pick up that pitcher!" replied Bessie, and she began to apply herself to the feat of climbing from the top berth, difficult enough when everything was slanting. Before she reached the ground there was a loud smash; the thick crockery pitcher itself had put an end to its wild career by banging against a projecting corner of iron.

Bessie's feet alighted on the damp carpet. "It is wet, very wet," she remarked, "still it is odd there should have been so much water left in the pitcher." She piled all the clothes she could lay hold of securely in the upper berth, and then after drying her feet, curled herself in such blankets as she could find, and was soon asleep; for the storm subsided as suddenly as it had arisen. The morning was bright and clear. The party had not suffered from the storm except that the hats of the ladies were a little limp from their squabble with the pitcher.

THE SIGNAL.

It was near noon when they came to the familiar port of Marseilles. There were the crowded quay, a boy in wooden shoes waving his signal, the line of large vessels, the swarm of small boats, the row of friends awaiting the arrival of the steamer, and among them, eagerly pressing to the best place, were Mrs. Horner, Mary and Mr. Hervey.

Long before they met, they waved handkerchiefs and called out words of joy and welcome, all unintelligible to the ear, but well understood by the heart.

Mr. Hervey was the first person to reach them. As they stepped on shore, he seized Bessie's hand, and bending over her, whispered:

"Will you bid me welcome as a new brother?"

MARSEILLES AGAIN.

www.ingramcontent.com/pod-product-compliance
Lightning Source LLC
Chambersburg PA
CBHW020322240426
43673CB00039B/892